The Master Key
to
Understanding
the Bible

The Master Key to Understanding the Bible

ISBN: 978-0-9829954-3-3

Harpazo Publishing Company

Houston, Texas

Author: Paul Felter, PhD

All Scripture passages from Public Domain King James Bible

Table of Contents

PREFACE   5

CHAPTER ONE – FAITH OR WORKS?   7

CHAPTER TWO – ENTER RIGHT DIVISION.   9

CHAPTER THREE – TIME PAST, GENESIS TO MALACHI 13

CHAPTER FOUR – TIME PAST, MATTHEW TO JOHN   15

CHAPTER FIVE – TIME PAST, ACTS CHAPTERS 1-7   19

CHAPTER SIX – BUT NOW, THE CHURCH AGE   33

CHAPTER SEVEN – THE FALL OF ISRAEL   37

CHAPTER EIGHT – THE LITTLE FLOCK EXPLAINED   39

CHAPTER NINE – AGES TO COME 43

CHAPTER TEN – THE BOOK OF REVELATION   51

CHAPTER ELEVEN – CONCLUSION 63

Preface

Decades ago, when I was saved, I started studying the Bible with a heartfelt desire to understand God's Word. But as I progressed, I found several passages that seemed to contradict. Everything in the Old Testament harmonized as that pertains mostly to Israel.

But the New Testament was a different story. The four gospels, Matthew, Mark, Luke, and John mirrored the Old Testament. The scene was Israel, Jerusalem, the Temple, the priesthood, and the feast days. But the epistles of Paul, Romans thru Philemon, seem to be almost out of sync with the rest of the Bible. Paul emphasized grace, everyone else encouraged works, the keeping of the commandments.

I was told, as you probably were too, that the Old Testament was written to the Jews and the New Testament to the Church. If that were true, then why was I having so many issues?

In addition to emphasizing the keeping of the commandments, most New Testament writers spoke of the coming kingdom and the last days as imminent. This did not make sense. Didn't they know there was a long church age coming and the last days were 2000 years away? I could not rationalize these inconsistencies and paradoxical passages. Since I did not know what to do and none of my pastors or teachers seemed to know either, I just spiritualized or ignored those difficult sections of the Bible.

The serious student of the Bible cannot help but notice that Jesus and His disciples frequently stressed keeping the commandments of the Law of Moses. Here are some familiar examples.

*"And he said unto him, Why callest thou me good? there is none good but one, that is, God: but if thou wilt enter into life, **keep the commandments**." - Matthew 19:17*

*"If ye love me, **keep my commandments**." - John 14:15*

*"And hereby we do know that we know him, if we **keep his commandments**. He that saith, I know him, and keepeth not his commandments, is a liar, and the truth is not in him." – 1st John 2:3-4*

*"Here is the patience of the saints: here are they that **keep the commandments** of God, and the faith of Jesus." - Revelation 14:12*

Many more passages stress the keeping of the commandments. But Paul teaches salvation by grace through faith and not of works. That by works, keeping the commandments of the law of Moses, shall no man be justified in God's sight.

"Therefore, by the deeds of the law there shall no flesh be justified in his sight: for by the law is the knowledge of sin." - Romans 3:20

The contradiction is clear.

The book of James declares works, the keeping of the commandments, part of the process of justification. From James' point of view, salvation is by faith plus works. This is contradictory to Paul's salvation by grace through faith and not of works.

I labored with this and several other issues churning in the back of my mind for many years. Pastors and teachers would do their best to harmonize Paul's doctrine of grace with James' doctrine of works. Frequently I was amazed and entertained at the length's they would go to force harmony between Paul and James. But there truly is no harmony. What could I do? I finally found the answer to the conundrum.

The apostle Paul commanded Timothy to rightly divide the Word of Truth. By rightly dividing the word of Truth all the troubling issues disappeared. Right division is the process of determining the correct audience for each chapter and book of the Bible for doctrine. The Bible contains much doctrine, but it is not all our doctrine. God dealt with Israel before the Church, the body of Christ, began. He will deal with Israel again after the dispensation of Grace ends with the Rapture of the church. Israel has their doctrine and we, the church, have ours. Another way of stating this concept as it applies to the church; "the Bible was written FOR us, but not all written TO us." Israel has their truth, and we have ours.

That is why I authored this book. I know that other students of the Word have similar issues, easily corrected by following Paul's command. I believe this teaching of right division should be the basic, introductory teaching for all new Christians, so they do not labor for years under erroneous church traditions created by mere men masquerading as proper Christian doctrine.

Right division is truly a liberating study. Finally, we can put the entire word of God into proper perspective. We know exactly what writings apply directly to the church, the Body of Christ, and what books apply to Israel. The reason we have so many denominations and teachings in the church is that pastors, teachers, professors, Bible colleges, and Seminaries do not teach right division. If they taught right division, there would be true unity of doctrine and truth in the Body of Christ.

There are three basic questions of right division we must answer for each chapter and book of the Bible. Only then can we grasp the intended meaning and proper application of the passage.

1. Who is speaking?
2. Who is the intended audience?
3. What is the timeframe or setting?

Answering these questions when studying the Bible is critical. The most important question being who is the intended audience. When we know the intended audience of a passage, chapter, or book of the Bible, we can then correctly apply the passage. In other words, when Jesus spoke to Israel during His earthly ministry, He is not speaking to the Body of Christ, He is speaking to Israel. When Peter condemns Israel for crucifying their Messiah Jesus in Acts chapter 2, he is not speaking to the Body of Christ, he is speaking to Israel.

Once you determine the intended audience of any passage of scripture, your understanding of the Bible is greatly enhanced. You will know what books apply to Israel and what books apply to us, the Body of Christ. Previous areas of confusion or contradiction will disappear. That is the purpose of this book, to help you make that determination.

Follow along with me in this study with an open mind to the Scriptures. For it is God's Word that is alive, powerful, and sharper than a two-edged sword. Read each Bible passage in its entirety and let the Bible speak for itself.

Read carefully and slowly, "**that I may shew thee the word of God**." 1 Samuel 9:27.

Chapter One - Faith or Works?

Why do all denominations affirm their doctrines as the truth, yet many such dogmas are contradictory?

Denominations within Christianity exist because churches and groups place unwarranted emphasis on scripture passages having little if any application to this present dispensation of grace, the Church, the Body of Christ. The misapplication of Scripture, a favorite device of Satan, creates much error, false doctrines, and confusion within the church. It is the foremost problem within Christianity, especially in America.

Why does the Apostle Paul teach justification by grace through faith, but James teaches justification by works?

The dichotomy between Paul's doctrine of grace and James' doctrine of works is the continuing controversy of law and grace. Does the law apply to the dispensation of grace, the current Gentile church age? Since Gentiles were never under the Law of Moses, works of the Law cannot be a requirement for Gentile salvation. James was a Jew living under the Law writing to Jews. Works of the Law were an integral part of their relationship with God.

The apostle Paul frequently wrote about Justification by grace through faith. He makes a clear distinction between grace and works of the law. They are mutually exclusive. One cannot be under both doctrines simultaneously. Works accrue merited favor or wages. Faith by grace earns nothing as it is unmerited favor. Here are a few passages on justification by faith.

*"Therefore, we conclude that a man is **justified by faith** without the deeds of the law."* - Romans 3:28

*"Therefore, being **justified by faith**, we have peace with God through our Lord Jesus Christ:"* - Romans 5:1

*"But that no man is justified by the law in the sight of God, it is evident: for, **The just shall live by faith**."* - Galatians 3:11

*"For if Abraham were justified by works, he hath whereof to glory; but not before God. For what saith the scripture? **Abraham believed God, and it was counted unto him for righteousness.**"* - Romans 4:2-3

Works and the Commandments

James, the half-brother of Jesus, writes in his epistle much about works. He states that the works of the Law, the keeping the commandments of the Law of Moses, are essential to justification or salvation. The following are some examples of James' teaching.

*"What doth it profit, my brethren, though a man say he hath faith, and have not works? **can faith save him?**"* - James 2:14

*"But wilt thou know, O vain man, that **faith without works is dead**? Was not Abraham our father **justified by works**, when he had offered Isaac his son upon the altar?" - James 2:20-21*

*"Ye see then how that **by works a man is justified**, and **not by faith only**." - James 2:24*

In the gospels, Jesus commanded His followers to keep the commandments. He spoke the following:

*"And he said unto him, Why callest thou me good? there is none good but one, that is, God: but if thou wilt enter into life, **keep the commandments**." - Matthew 19:17*

*"If ye love me, **keep my commandments**." - John 14:15*

*"He that **hath my commandments, and keepeth them**, he it is that loveth me: and he that loveth me shall be loved of my Father, and I will love him, and will manifest myself to him." - John 14:21*

*"If ye **keep my commandments**, ye shall abide in my love; even as I have kept my Father's commandments and abide in his love." - John 15:10*

Was Jesus mistaken? Absolutely not! Jesus was born, lived, and died on the cross under the law of Moses. In compliance with the Law of Moses, Jesus instructed Jews to keep the commandments of the law. In the Old Testament, God gave instructions to the Jews to keep the commandments of the law. God repeated these instructions over three hundred times through Moses and the Prophets. The apostle John mirrored Jesus' instructions.

*"And hereby we do know that we know him, if we **keep his commandments**. He that saith, I know him, and keepeth not his commandments, is a liar, and the truth is not in him." – 1ˢᵗ John 2:3-4*

*"By this we know that we love the children of God, when we love God, and **keep his commandments**." – 1ˢᵗ John 5:2*

These are but a few examples of passages that proclaim salvation and justification by keeping the commandments, the works of the Law of Moses. The teachings of Jesus, Peter, James, and John harmonize with justification by faith plus works. The entire Old Testament instructs Israel to keep the commandments of the Lord. So, the apostle Paul alone proclaims salvation by Grace through Faith, not by the works of the Law.

*"For by **grace are ye saved through faith**; and that not of yourselves: it is the gift of God: **Not of works**, lest any man should boast." - Ephesians 2:8-9*

The contradiction is clear. Paul teaches grace through faith. James and everyone else teaches a faith plus works-based justification requiring the keeping of the commandments.

These two concepts of salvation are incompatible. They cannot coexist as requirements for salvation because grace is unmerited favor while works are earned favor. These doctrines are opposites.

Here we see one of the many confusing issues in the Bible. Since all the previous passages are from the New Testament, what can we do? We have been taught that the New Testament was written to the Church, right? Is that true? If so, then we have a fundamental problem with the Bible.

Do we try to spiritualize these passages to force harmony? If we do, we rob the scriptures of their true meaning and force upon them man's doctrines and traditional dogma. But this is what most pastors and teachers do. They alter the literal meaning of a passage in an attempt at harmony. Many other teachers simply ignore difficult passages sidestepping the issues altogether. Lay people do the same. They either skim over the difficult passages or ignore them.

Chapter Two - Enter Right Division.

The Apostle Paul gives us the answer to the faith-works conundrum in the following passage:

*"**Study** to show thyself approved unto God, a workman that needeth not to be ashamed, **rightly dividing the word of truth**." – 2nd Timothy 2:15*

Let's deconstruct this passage.

1. Paul commands that we **study** to be approved by the Lord when we stand before Him at the judgment seat of Christ. If we do not study, we will be ashamed before Him. Who wants to be ashamed when standing before Jesus? No one, I would hope.
2. Paul then gives us the **method** of study. We are to "rightly divide the word of truth." Rightly divide means to "cut straight". When you cut something straight, like a cantaloupe or watermelon, you divide it into useable individual portions. The same concept applies to rightly dividing the word of truth. We divide it into sections that apply to specific audiences. There is truth for those that came before the Church, and truth for those that will come after the removal of the Church from the earth. Paul tells us to divide truth from truth.

Not only does Paul command us to study and give us the method of study, right division. He reveals the application of the method in Ephesians Chapter 2. Shortly we will explore how Paul "rightly divides the word of truth."

The apostle also wrote:

*"All scripture is given by **inspiration of God**, and is profitable for **doctrine**, for reproof, for correction, for instruction in righteousness:" - 2Tim 3:16*

God inspired every word of your King James Bible. The entire Bible is profitable for our study. We need to have a working knowledge of the entire Word of God. However, only a portion was written directly to us, the Body of Christ. Those books and passages are where we derive church doctrine and instruction on how to live the Christian life. The Bible was written for our learning and edification. But not all for our doctrine and instruction for living. Not understanding this truth is what causes the numerous denominational differences and lack of unity among the brethren. To understand how to live the Christian life you might start in Philippians, not Matthew. In Matthew Jesus instructs Jews under the Law of Moses on how to live in the coming kingdom. Jesus preached; "repent for the kingdom of heaven is at hand."

Right Division Example

Before we look at Ephesians chapter 2, Let's read how Jesus rightly divided the word of truth in Luke's gospel, chapter 4. The setting is Jesus at the synagogue in Nazareth reading from chapter 61 of Isaiah.

"The Spirit of the Lord is upon me, because he hath anointed me to preach the gospel to the poor; he hath sent me to heal the brokenhearted, to preach deliverance to the captives, and recovering of sight to the blind, to set at liberty them that are bruised, **To preach the acceptable year of the Lord***. And he* **closed the book***, and he gave it again to the minister and sat down. And the eyes of all them that were in the synagogue were fastened on him. And he began to say unto them,* **This day is this scripture fulfilled in your ears***." - Luke 4:18-21*

Jesus stopped reading Isaiah 61 with the phrase "**To preach the acceptable year of the Lord**." But notice in Isaiah chapter 61 that the passage continues for several verses.

"To proclaim the acceptable year of the LORD, and **the day of vengeance of our God***; to comfort all that mourn; To appoint unto them that mourn in Zion, to give unto them beauty for ashes, the oil of joy for mourning, the garment of praise for the spirit of heaviness; that they might be called trees of righteousness, the planting of the LORD, that he might be glorified." - Isaiah 61:2-3*

Jesus did not read "the day of vengeance of our God" because His first coming was for salvation, not vengeance. His second coming at the end of the 7-year Tribulation will be in vengeance and wrath executing judgment upon a Christ-rejecting Israel, the Antichrist, and world.

Jesus rightly divided this passage into His first coming and second coming. Two separate missions, one of grace and mercy, the other of vengeance and wrath. An excellent example of right division from our Lord Jesus Christ.

In Ephesians Ch. 2 Paul divides the word of truth into 3 general time periods.

1. Time Past
2. But Now
3. Ages to Come

The "But Now" time period is this present "dispensation of grace" that began with the apostle Paul and will end at the Rapture of the church. The "Time Past" period is everything before the dispensation of grace from Genesis to the early chapters of Acts. The "Ages to Come" period is everything after the dispensation of grace ends, beginning with the 7-year Tribulation through the book of Revelation. Let's take a quick look at these three divisions as found in Ephesians chapter 2.

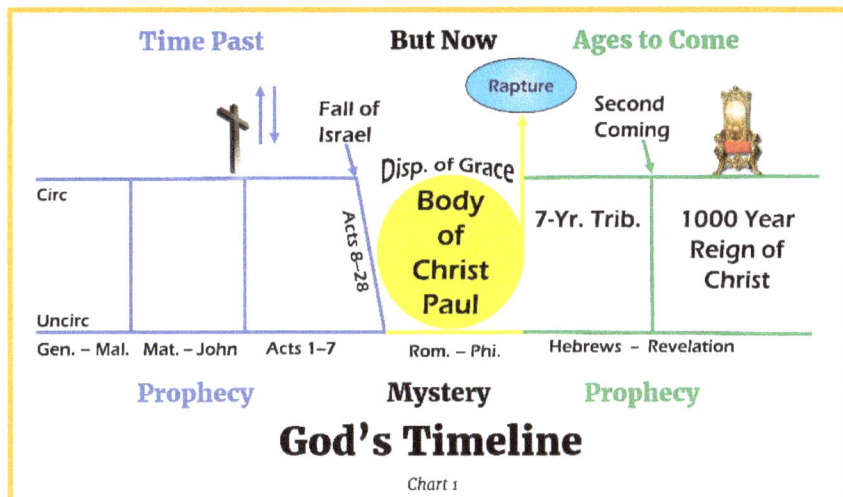

God's Timeline

Chart 1

1. Time Past

*"Wherefore remember, that ye being in **time past** Gentiles in the flesh, who are called Uncircumcision by that which is called the Circumcision in the flesh made by hands; That at that time ye were without Christ, being aliens from the commonwealth of Israel, and strangers from the covenants of promise, having no hope, and without God in the world:" - Ephesians 2:11-12*

Paul is writing to the believers at Ephesus who are mostly Gentiles. In this passage, he reminds them that in "**time past**" they were called the "Uncircumcision". They and all Gentiles before them were "without Christ", "aliens" and "strangers" from Israel and the promises. They had "no hope" and were "without God in the world." Gentiles were not the recipients of the promises given to Abraham and the Law of Moses. In the Antediluvian world and even after Noah's flood, Gentiles were godless pagans with few exceptions. God wanted a people that would worship and obey Him, so He called Abram from Ur of the Chaldees as the patriarch of His chosen people. Much of the "**time past**" period proclaims the journey of Israel from slavery in Egypt to the glory days of King David and Solomon to the captivity in Babylon, a new Temple, and to the ministry of Jesus of Nazareth.

Gentiles in "**time past**" had no possibility of salvation unless they converted to Judaism, were circumcised, and kept the Law of Moses. Those Gentiles were called proselytes. Most Gentiles in "**time past**" were pagans with no hope. Jesus said the following while speaking with the woman at Jacob's well:

*"Ye worship ye know not what: we know what we worship: **for salvation is of the Jews**." - John 4:22 KJV*

2. But Now

*"**But now** in Christ Jesus ye who sometimes were far off are made nigh by the blood of Christ. For he is our peace, who hath made both one, and hath **broken down the middle wall of partition** between us; Having abolished in his flesh the enmity, even the law of commandments contained in ordinances; for to make in himself of twain **one new man**, so making peace; And that he might*

reconcile both unto God in one body by the cross, having slain the enmity thereby: And came and preached peace to you which were afar off, and to them that were nigh." - Ephesians 2:13-17

The "**But now**" division is the present church age, the dispensation of Grace, the Body of Christ, the one new man. The "But Now" period ends with the rapture of the church. Gentiles can now come to God through the "blood of Christ", no need to convert to Judaism. In the Body of Christ, there is no difference between Jew and Gentile since we together are "one new man." Both reconciled to God "by the cross." The "middle wall of partition" between Jew and Gentile was "broken down" at the cross.

Previously in "**time past**" a clear distinction between Jew, the circumcision, and Gentile, the uncircumcision, existed. But now that distinction has been "broken down", it does not exist in the Body of Christ; a critical distinction between the Body of Christ and all things pertaining to Israel.

3. Ages to Come

*"That in the **ages to come** he might show the exceeding riches of his grace in his kindness toward us through Christ Jesus." - Eph 2:7*

In "**ages to come**" the riches of His grace will shine to all that believe, both in heaven and on earth.

"Time past", "But now" and "ages to come", a simple division of the word of Truth. The past, present, and future. Like the division of our lives. We all have a past, a present, and a future. Let's take a closer look at the "time past" period of the Bible.

Chapter Three – Time Past, Genesis to Malachi

The "time past" timeline begins with Genesis and continues through the early chapters of Acts. The first section for our discussion is Genesis to Malachi, the Old Testament.

Genesis to Malachi

For our "rightly dividing" study we must determine if the "Middle Wall of Partition" exists between Jew, the circumcision, and Gentile, the uncircumcision. If it is present, when did it start? Does the "Middle Wall of Partition" continue to the end of the Old Testament or does it stop at some point? This determination enables us to rightly divide the Old Testament determining the appropriate audience to whom God was speaking. Here is a quick, birds-eye view of the Old Testament.

- After the fall of Adam, mankind declined because of sin. God destroyed mankind with a global flood except for Noah and his family.
- After Noah came the tower of Babel. Mankind was still in rebellion against God.
- In the early chapters of Genesis all were pagans. The entire world was Gentile.
- God makes a covenant with Abraham. The covenant includes blessings, a land, and a nation.
- The sign of this covenant was circumcision.
- From this point forward there would be a difference between the circumcision (Israel) and the uncircumcision (Gentiles).
- Isaac, Jacob, and the 12 sons or tribes follow.
- They go to Egypt to escape a famine. There they become a great nation, Israel.
- Moses led Israel in the Exodus from Egypt and God gave him the Law on Mt. Sinai.
- Later came King David, Solomon, and the first Temple.
- After many Kings of Israel and Judah comes captivity in Assyria and Babylon.
- The Second Temple was built.
- The remainder of the Old Testament is the Prophets of Israel.

I told you that would be quick. So, when did the separation between Jew and Gentile begin?

In Exodus, we read that God put a difference between the Jew and the Egyptian (Gentiles).

*"And there shall be a great cry throughout all the land of Egypt, such as there was none like it, nor shall be like it anymore. But against any of the children of Israel shall not a dog move his tongue, against man or beast: that ye may know how that **the LORD doth put a difference between the Egyptians and Israel**." – Exodus 11:6-7*

In Leviticus, the Law, God makes a clear distinction between the Jew and Gentile.

*"And ye shall be holy unto me: for I the LORD am holy, and have **severed you from other people**, that ye should be mine." – Leviticus 20:26*

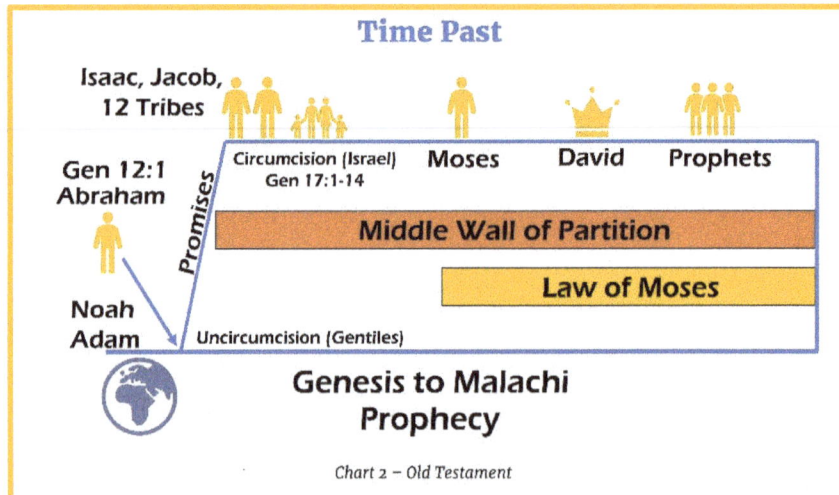

Chart 2 – Old Testament

The "Middle Wall of Partition", as Paul calls it in Ephesians chapter 2, clearly exists between Israel and Gentile nations in the Old Testament. God established this "Middle Wall of Partition" with Abraham by the sign of circumcision. God mandated circumcision for all of Abraham's descendants, Israel. God confirmed the middle wall of partition through the Law given to Moses. Even with a cursory reading of the Old Testament, the separation of Jew and Gentile is clear.

Is the church, the Body of Christ present in the Old Testament?

The Church, the Body of Christ, is not represented in the Old Testament since the "Middle Wall of Partition" is present. The church cannot exist in the Old Testament while a God-mandated distinction between Jew and Gentile prevails. Therefore, doctrine for the Body of Christ is not found in the Old Testament teachings. However, we do study the Old Testament for historical, spiritual, and prophetic reasons, but not for church doctrine.

Without a modicum of understanding of the Old Testament, one will not understand the setting and message of the four gospels. Instructions on how to live the Christian life under grace are not found in the Old Testament as Israel is under the Law of Moses and we are not. Many passages in the Old Testament speak to the greatness of God and are profitable for us, but the Old Testament is not the pattern for our Christian life and walk.

Answers to the basic right division questions.

1. Who is speaking? The primary voice in the Old Testament is God speaking through the fathers and prophets of Israel.
2. Who is the intended audience? Israel, as they are the recipients of the promises of Abraham and the Law of Moses.
3. What is the timeframe or setting? God calling a people to himself from Abraham through the prophet Malachi, the nation of Israel.

Chapter Four – Time Past, Matthew to John

The next section for review is Matthew through John, the four Gospels. We need to answer two additional questions.

1. What was the ministry of Jesus?

2. Was the "Middle Wall of Partition" still present between Jew and Gentile?

Matthew thru John begins with John the Baptist in Matthew chapter 3 and Jesus in Matthew chapter 4. Both preach the gospel of the kingdom, "repent, for the kingdom of heaven is at hand." Soon Jesus chooses His disciples and they also preach the gospel of the kingdom. What kingdom? The kingdom promised to Israel in the Old Testament. The kingdom for Israel was promised to Abraham, Moses, and King David. This kingdom would extend from the Nile River in Egypt to the River Euphrates in modern-day Iraq, Syria, and Turkey. They have yet to rule over that entire land area, but someday, with the help of their Messiah Jesus Christ, all that region will be theirs.

Question: What was the purpose of Jesus' earthly ministry?

Jesus himself tells us his purpose in Matthew chapter 15.

*"Then Jesus went thence, and departed into the coasts of Tyre and Sidon. And, behold, a woman of Canaan came out of the same coasts, and cried unto him, saying, Have mercy on me, O Lord, thou Son of David; my daughter is grievously vexed with a devil. But **he answered her not a word**. And his disciples came and besought him, saying, Send her away; for she crieth after us. But he answered and said**, I am not sent but unto the lost sheep of the house of Israel**." – Matthew 15:21-24*

In this passage, a Gentile "woman of Canaan" wants Jesus to heal her daughter. Both Jesus and the disciples want nothing to do with her. But her persistence and faith drive her into Jesus' immediate presence. Then Jesus proclaims to her "**I am not sent but unto the lost sheep of the house of Israel**." Here, in Jesus' own words, He clearly states that His earthly ministry is only to Israel, the Jews. What could be more clear?

The apostle Paul also tells us the purpose of Jesus' earthly ministry.

*"Now I say that Jesus Christ was **a minister of the circumcision** for the truth of God, to confirm the promises made unto the fathers:" – Romans 15:8*

Jesus came to minister to the "circumcision", Israel. He came to present himself as their Messiah and offer them the kingdom. This was the promise made to the "fathers", Abraham, Isaac, Jacob, etc. Even though Jesus died on the cross for the sin of the world both Jew and Gentile, His earthly ministry was to the Jews only. Jesus made that perfectly clear.

When Jesus sent out the 12 disciples to preach the gospel of the kingdom in Matthew Ch. 10, we read.

*"These twelve Jesus sent forth, and commanded them, saying, Go not into the way of the Gentiles, and into any city of the Samaritans enter ye not: **But go rather to the lost sheep of the house of Israel**. And as ye go, preach, saying, The kingdom of heaven is at hand." - Matthew 10:5-7*

Jesus commands His disciples not to go to the Gentiles but only to the "**lost sheep of the house of Israel**" preaching the "gospel of the kingdom", a gospel unique to Israel as God promised a kingdom to the fathers of Israel, not to Gentiles.

Here are a few more passages from the book of Matthew to show that Jesus was ministering to Israel, not Gentiles.

*"Whosoever therefore shall break one of these least commandments, and shall teach men so, he shall be called the least in the **kingdom of heaven**: but whosoever shall do and teach them, the same shall be called great in the **kingdom of heaven**. For I say unto you, That except your righteousness shall exceed the righteousness of the scribes and Pharisees, ye shall in no case enter into the **kingdom of heaven**." - Matthew 5:19-20 KJV*

We do not teach believers to keep the commandments so they can be called great in the kingdom of heaven. We are not under the Law of Moses and the "kingdom of heaven" is the earthly kingdom promised to Israel, not Gentiles. Also, our righteousness is the righteousness of Jesus Christ. We certainly do not compare ourselves to scribes and Pharisees under the Law of Moses. The above passage is purely for Israel and has no application to us, the church.

Another interesting verse from Matthew chapter 5.

*"But I say unto you, That whosoever is angry with his brother without a cause shall be in danger of the judgment: and whosoever shall say to his brother, Raca, shall be in danger of the council: but whosoever shall say, **Thou fool, shall be in danger of hell fire**." - Matthew 5:22 KJV*

Jesus said that if one calls a brother a "fool" he is in danger of "hell fire." But here is what our apostle Paul said to the believers at Galatia.

*"O **foolish** Galatians, who hath bewitched you, that ye should not obey the truth, before whose eyes Jesus Christ hath been evidently set forth, crucified among you? ... Are ye so **foolish**? having begun in the Spirit, are ye now made perfect by the flesh?" - Galatians 3:1, 3 KJV*

So, is the apostle Paul in danger of "hell fire?" I think not. Jesus was speaking to Israel under the Law in Matthew 5:22. Paul is writing to the body of Christ under grace. Two different paradigms, two different audiences, two different doctrines, one of law, the other of grace.

*"And if thy right eye offend thee, **pluck it out**, and cast it from thee: for it is profitable for thee that one of thy members should perish, and not that thy whole body should be cast into hell. And if thy right hand offend thee, **cut it off**, and cast it from thee: for it is profitable for thee that one of thy members should perish, and not that thy whole body should be cast into hell." - Matthew 5:29-30 KJV*

The only possible audience for this verse is Israel under the Law. We, the church, are under grace. Our salvation is not dependent on whether we lose an eye or a hand. That is not our pattern for Christian living. I have yet to a church named "The First Church of the One-Eyed Lefties." Simple faith is all that is required.

Another example.

"For if ye forgive men their trespasses, your heavenly Father will also forgive you: But if ye forgive not men their trespasses, neither will your Father forgive your trespasses." - Matthew 6:14-15 KJV

In the church, our forgiveness of sin is based solely on our faith in the finished work of Jesus Christ on the cross. He shed His blood as payment in full for sin and we appropriate that payment when we believe the gospel of grace. Jesus died for our sin, was buried, and rose again the third day according to the scriptures, 1st Corinthians 15:1-4. Our forgiveness by God is not conditional on our forgiveness of others.

And finally.

"And Jesus said unto them, Verily I say unto you, That ye which have followed me, in the regeneration when the Son of man shall sit in the throne of his glory, ye also shall sit upon twelve thrones, judging the twelve tribes of Israel." - Matthew 19:28 KJV

Jesus announces to His disciples that in the kingdom, the Millennial Reign, He will sit on "the throne of his glory." The disciples will also sit on "twelve thrones judging the twelve tribes of Israel." The disciples will Judge Israel, they will not judge Gentiles.

Jesus and the disciples are ministering only to the Jews. The "Middle Wall of Partition" is still in full effect during Jesus' ministry as recorded in the gospels.

The Law of Moses is operational in the gospels, as Paul writes:

*"But when the fulness of the time was come, God sent forth his Son, made of a woman, **made under the law**, To redeem them that were **under the law**, that we might receive the adoption of sons." - Galatians 4:4-5*

Jesus was born under the Law of Moses. He lived and died on the cross under the Law of Moses. Jesus died under the Law to "redeem them that were under the Law", Israel. He also died for us, that we Gentiles "might receive the adoption of sons." There is no need for the adoption of Jews, as they are by birth the children of God. They are God's son. God spoke to Moses about what he should say to Pharaoh.

*"And thou shalt say unto Pharaoh, Thus saith the LORD, **Israel is my son, even my firstborn**:" - Exodus 4:22 KJV*

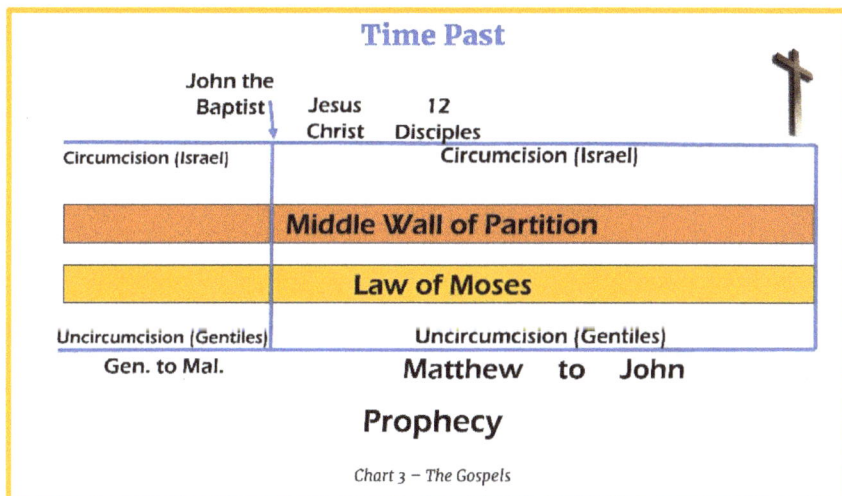

Chart 3 – The Gospels

Continuing in Matthew, Jesus said:

*"Think not that I am come to destroy the law, or the prophets: I am not come to destroy, but **to fulfill**." - Matthew 5:17*

Jesus came to fulfill the Law of Moses. Therefore, it was in full operation during His earthly ministry.

Summary

The "Middle Wall of Partition" was in effect during the earthly ministry of Jesus Christ. A clear distinction exists between Jew and Gentile in the four gospels.

Does the church, the Body of Christ, exist during the ministry of Jesus and the apostles?

Since the "Middle Wall of Partition" is present in the gospels, the Church, the Body of Christ cannot yet exist, as the Body of Christ has no distinction between Jew and Gentile.

Who is Jesus addressing in Matthew thru John?

Jesus' ministry was solely to Israel, the Jews, not Gentiles, and not the Body of Christ.

The "Middle Wall of Partition" clearly exists in the Old Testament and the Gospels.

Answers to the basic right division questions.

1. Who is speaking? The primary voice in the gospels is Jesus Christ speaking through the writers.
2. Who is the intended audience? Israel, the Jews are the intended audience as no one had a ministry to Gentiles.
3. What is the timeframe or setting? The setting has not changed from the Old Testament. Galilee, Jerusalem, the Temple, the priesthood, sacrifices, and the feast days. Israel under the Law of Moses. Jesus ministering to Jews and fulfilling Old Testament prophecy about His first coming.

Chapter Five - Time Past, Acts Chapters 1-7

Are the "Middle Wall of Partition" and the Law of Moses still in force in the early chapters of Acts? The correct answer is critical to properly understanding the Bible. If they are still in effect then the church, the Body of Christ cannot be present.

Before we examine Acts chapters 1-7, we must learn a parable given by Jesus that explains the purpose of the first seven chapters of Acts.

*"He spake also this parable; A certain man had a **fig tree** planted in his vineyard; and he came and **sought fruit thereon and found none**. Then said he unto the dresser of his vineyard, Behold, these **three years** I come seeking fruit on this fig tree, and **find none: cut it down**; why cumbereth it the ground? And he answering said unto him, Lord, **let it alone this year also**, till I shall dig about it, and dung it: **And if it bear fruit, well: and if not, then after that thou shalt cut it down**." - Luke 13:6-9*

The parable is not difficult to follow. Here is the simple, straight forward meaning.

- The "fig tree" is Israel.
- God planted the "fig tree" in His vineyard, earth.
- Jesus visits the "fig tree", Israel, and finds no fruit; they reject Him as Messiah.
- For 3 years, the duration of His earthly ministry, Jesus is looking for fruit, acceptance of Him as Messiah, but finds none.
- Jesus says, "cut it down", it's a burden to the ground.
- God the Father, the dresser, says to give it another year and He will work it.
- If it does not bear fruit by then, "cut it down".

How does the parable of the fig tree play out? Israel, the fig tree, is given a one-year extension of mercy to accept Jesus as their Messiah. From Pentecost in Acts chapter 2 to Stephen testifying before the Jewish council in Acts chapter 7. If Israel does not accept Jesus as Messiah, they will be "cut down" as a nation.

Let's look at some passages to determine if Gentiles or the Body of Christ are present in the first seven chapters of Acts.

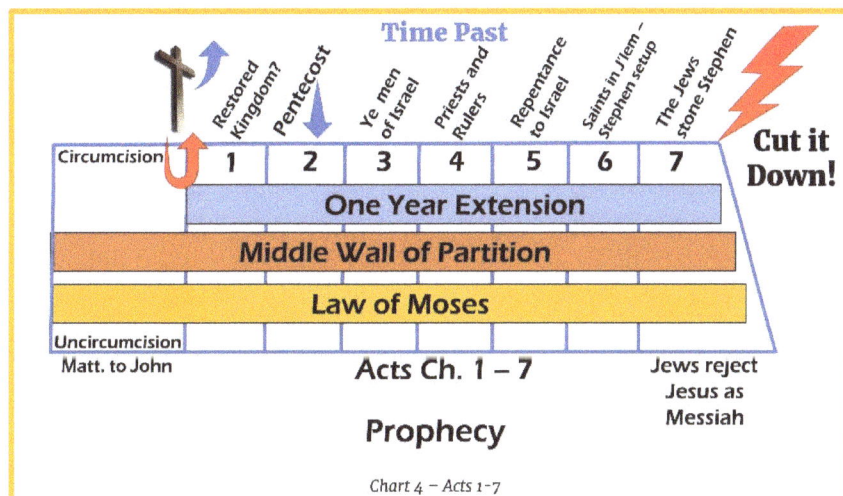

Chart 4 – Acts 1-7

Acts Chapter 1.

The events of Acts chapter 1 are entirely Jewish, not a Gentile in sight. Jesus speaks with the eleven remaining disciples about the kingdom and commanded them to remain in Jerusalem until the Holy Spirit should come. Then Jesus ascended into heaven. I believe this was a sad moment. The disciples had been with Jesus for three years. They witnessed many miracles, the sick healed, lepers cleansed, and the dead raised. Then to see Jesus whipped, beaten, and crucified was devastating. They had given up everything to follow Jesus, now he was dead. But then, the miracle of miracles, He was alive again. He had risen from the dead, just as He prophesied. Since Jesus was victorious over death proving He was the Son of God, defeating Rome should be no problem. Hence the following question.

"When they therefore were come together, they asked of him, saying, Lord, wilt thou at this time restore again the kingdom to Israel?" - Acts 1:6

Just before Jesus' ascension, Peter asked the Lord if He would, at that time, restore the promised kingdom to Israel, bring back the glory days of King David. This was a reasonable question as they have been preaching the gospel of the Kingdom for three years. Since the kingdom was promised to Israel and not Gentiles, the distinction between Jew and Gentile is still present here in Acts chapter one.

Judas had committed suicide leaving vacant an apostleship. The eleven gathered in Jerusalem to elect Judas' replacement.

"For it is written in the book of Psalms, Let his habitation be desolate, and let no man dwell therein: and his bishoprick let another take." - Acts 1:20 KJV

The eleven disciples chose Matthias to replace Judas. Why was a replacement necessary? There are twelve tribes of Israel. There must be twelve apostles to Israel, one for each tribe, one for each throne to judge the tribes.

Acts Chapter 2

The day of Pentecost. Jews had been celebrating Pentecost for centuries. The holy day commemorated the giving of God's Law to Moses on Mount Sinai after the exodus from Egypt. This feast required Jews from the entire region to come to Jerusalem to honor the Lord. The twelve disciples were in a house waiting with great anticipation for the promise of the Holy Spirit. The promise was fulfilled as the Holy Spirit fell on the disciples and they began to speak with "other tongues," the languages of the multitude of Jews present in Jerusalem that day.

Who was there that day?

*"And there were dwelling at Jerusalem **Jews**, devout men, **out of every nation under heaven**." - Acts 2:5*

There were present at the feast of Pentecost that day Jews "out of every nation under heaven." All nations that had a Jewish population, however small, had sent representatives to Jerusalem for this Pentecost.

*"And how hear we every man in our own tongue, wherein we were born? Parthians, and Medes, and Elamites, and the dwellers in Mesopotamia, and in Judaea, and Cappadocia, in Pontus, and Asia, Phrygia, and Pamphylia, in Egypt, and in the parts of Libya about Cyrene, and strangers of Rome, **Jews, and proselytes**, Cretes and Arabians, we do hear them speak in our tongues the wonderful works of God." – Acts 2:8–11 KJV*

Jews and proselytes from every nation throughout the Middle East, Asia Minor, and Europe. The only Gentiles there were the proselytes, Gentiles that converted to Judaism.

*"But Peter, standing up with the eleven, lifted up his voice, and said unto them, **Ye men of Judaea, and all ye that dwell at Jerusalem**, be this known unto you, and hearken to my words:" – Act 2:14*

*"**Ye men of Israel**, hear these words; Jesus of Nazareth, a man approved of God among you by miracles and wonders and signs, which God did by him in the midst of you, as ye yourselves also know:" – Acts 2:22*

*"Therefore let all the **house of Israel** know assuredly, that God hath made that same Jesus, whom ye have crucified, both Lord and Christ." – Acts 2:36*

These verses clearly demonstrate that everyone at Pentecost that day were "Jews and proselytes." Any Gentiles present had previously converted to Judaism. There were no Gentiles present worshipping God as Gentiles. Pentecost is not a holy day for Gentiles. The distinction between Jew and Gentile is still present. Therefore, the church, the body of Christ, did not begin at Pentecost as church tradition proclaims. Let me develop this thought further.

The word "church" is the Greek word "ecclesia" which means "called out ones" or "assembly".

The mistake most Christians make is thinking that every time they read the word church in the New Testament the passage is speaking to us, the Body of Christ. Nothing could be further from the truth.

In the Septuagint, the Greek translation of the Old Testament written about 270 BC, the word church is found over 330 times referring to an assembly of Jews.

In the King James Old Testament, the Hebrew word for "assembly" is translated as "congregation". If you are familiar with the Old Testament, you have seen the word congregation many times.

The word church can be an assembly of Jews or Christians.

A fitting example from Stephen found in Acts chapter 7:38 refers to Moses and Israel after the Exodus from Egypt.

*"This is he, that was in the **church in the wilderness** with the angel which spake to him in the mount Sina, and with our fathers: who received the lively oracles to give unto us:"*

This is Moses receiving the Law from God at Mt. Sinai. Stephen refers to the tribes of Israel as the "church in the wilderness."

So, when you read the word "church" in the New Testament do not automatically assume the passage refers to us, the Body of Christ.

Now, concerning church tradition, we have a genuine problem. Church tradition is dogma passed down within the church over many centuries. Much of this dogma began with the church of Rome in the 4th century and we are still suffering from their errors today. Sadly, the reformation did not correct many of the erroneous doctrines of the Roman church. Also, many denominations have doctrines and beliefs passed down for centuries in their doctrinal teachings.

What did Jesus say about tradition?

*"And he said unto them, Full well **ye reject the commandment of God**, that ye may **keep your own tradition**. ... Making the **word of God of none effect through your tradition**, which ye have delivered: and many such like things do ye." Mark 7:9, 13 KJV*

Even in Jesus' time, the religious traditions of men usurped the true doctrine of God thus making "the word of God of none effect." In other words, when we in the Body of Christ follow the traditions of men masquerading as church doctrine, we nullify the effectual working power of the word of God. Much of the teaching from pulpits today is erroneous church tradition, not Biblical doctrine.

Church tradition is one of Satan's favorite modes of deception, keeping believers away from true Biblical wisdom and understanding all the while believing they are hearing and learning Biblical truth.

The idea that the church, the body of Christ, started in Acts chapter 2 with the coming of the Holy Spirit is one such church tradition. Let's carefully examine what happened in Acts chapter 2 and for what purpose.

If you visit most any mainstream Protestant church in America, they will tell you without equivocation that the present church, the body of Christ began in Acts chapter 2 with the coming of the Holy Spirit and that Peter preached the first sermon. That is what I was taught and that is what I taught for many years. But I always had questions that I could not rationalize like why is Peter preaching from the book of Joel about the last days? That never made sense to me, but all my pastors and teachers believed that was the beginning of the church age, so I just went along.

As we have read, everyone there at Pentecost was a Jew or proselyte, but most were not believers in Jesus as Messiah. When the Holy Spirit came, he fell upon the disciples only, not the crowd of people celebrating the holiday. Was the coming of the Holy Spirit prophesied in the Old Testament?

*"Thus saith the LORD that made thee, and formed thee from the womb, which will help thee; Fear not, O Jacob, my servant; and thou, Jesurun, whom I have chosen. For I will pour water upon him that is thirsty, and floods upon the dry ground: **I will pour my spirit upon thy seed**, and my blessing upon thine offspring: And they shall spring up as among the grass, as willows by the water courses." - Isa 44:2-4 KJV*

*"Until the **spirit be poured upon us from on high**, and the wilderness be a fruitful field, and the fruitful field be counted for a forest." - Isa 32:15 KJV*

Isaiah prophesied the pouring out of the Spirit upon Israel seven centuries before Pentecost.

Joel also prophesied the pouring out of the Holy Spirit.

*"And it shall come to pass afterward, that **I will pour out my spirit** upon all flesh; and your sons and your daughters shall prophesy, your old men shall dream dreams, your young men shall see visions: And also upon the servants and upon the handmaids in those days will **I pour out my spirit**." - Joel 2:28-29 KJV*

In Time Past the coming of the Holy Spirit was a National Promise to Israel that preceded the coming Kingdom. The pouring out of the Holy Spirit would give Israel power to endure the time of Jacob's trouble, the 70th week of Daniel's prophecy, the 7-year Tribulation.

The passage from Joel chapter 2 quoted by Peter in Acts 2:16-21 bears closer scrutiny.

*"But **this is that** which was spoken by the prophet Joel; And it shall come to pass in the **last days**, saith God, **I will pour out of my Spirit** upon all flesh: and your sons and your daughters shall prophesy, and your young men shall see visions, and your old men shall dream dreams: And on my servants and on my handmaidens **I will pour out in those days of my Spirit**; and they shall prophesy: And I will shew **wonders in heaven above**, and signs in the earth beneath; **blood, and fire, and vapor of smoke: The sun shall be turned into darkness, and the moon into blood**, before that great and notable day of the Lord come: And it shall come to pass, that **whosoever shall call on the name of the Lord shall be saved**." - Act 2:16-21 KJV*

Let's analyze this passage.

"But this is that which was spoken by the prophet Joel;" - Act 2:16

What is Peter referring to with the phrase "this is that"?

"this" is the outpouring of the Holy Spirit.

"that" is the prophecy in Joel chapter 2 of the outpouring of the Spirit just before the coming of the Kingdom; before the 7-year Tribulation, the 70th week of Daniel's prophecy. Also known as the time of Jacob's trouble, and the great and terrible Day of the Lord.

Peter is proclaiming to Israel and specifically to the Jews present that day at the feast of Pentecost, they are in the "last days."

"wonders in heaven, signs in the earth, fire, smoke, the sun turned to darkness, the moon into blood". These events prophesied by Joel occur during the 7-year Tribulation just before the second coming of Jesus Christ. These events occur "before that great and notable day of the Lord", the second coming of Jesus Christ.

Let's put this in number format for clarity:

1. The coming of the Holy Spirit is a fulfillment of the prophecy given by the prophets Isaiah and Joel.

2. The purpose of the filling of the Holy Spirit was to help Israel through the time of Jacob's trouble, the 7-year Tribulation also prophesied in Joel chapter 2.

3. Peter is proclaiming the beginning of the "last days" for Israel, the 7-year Tribulation.

4. Peter is NOT proclaiming the beginning of the Church, the Body of Christ!

But the "last days," the Time of Jacob's Trouble," and the second coming did not come, what happened? The dispensation of grace happened as I will explain shortly.

In Acts chapter 2 verse 22 we read:

*"Ye men of Israel, hear these words; Jesus of Nazareth, a man approved of God among you by miracles and wonders and signs, which God did by him in the midst of you, as ye yourselves also know: Him, being delivered by the determinate counsel and foreknowledge of God, ye have taken, and **by wicked hands have crucified and slain**:" - Act 2:22-23.*

What is Peter saying here? Is he preaching the gospel of grace? Is Peter preaching salvation by trusting that Jesus died for your sin, was buried, and rose again the third day? No, absolutely not!

Peter is chastising Israel for crucifying their Messiah. He is condemning Israel for the crucifixion, not preaching salvation through Jesus' death on the cross as payment for sin.

Peter then quotes King David in Psalm 16:8-11

*"I have set the LORD always before me: because he is at my right hand, I shall not be moved. Therefore my heart is glad, and my glory rejoiceth: my flesh also shall rest in hope. For thou wilt not leave my soul in hell; **neither wilt thou suffer thine Holy One to see corruption**. Thou wilt shew me the path of life: in thy presence is fulness of joy; at thy right hand there are pleasures for evermore."*

Peter is showing the Jews at Pentecost that Jesus is the fulfillment of the prophecy given by King David in Psalm 16 validating that Jesus is the Messiah. Specifically, the resurrection of Jesus wherein God did not "suffer thine Holy One to see corruption."

Many of those listening that day understood.

*"Now when they heard this, they were **pricked in their heart**, and said unto Peter and to the rest of the apostles, Men and brethren, **what shall we do**?" - Act 2:37 KJV*

Peter replies.

*"**Repent, and be baptized** every one of you in the name of Jesus Christ for the remission of sins, and ye shall receive the gift of the Holy Ghost." - Act 2:38 KJV*

Peter is following Jesus' command from Mark chapter 16 and Matthew chapter 28, commonly called the great commission.

*"Afterward he appeared unto **the eleven** as they sat at meat, and upbraided them with their unbelief and hardness of heart, because they believed not them which had seen him after he was risen. And he said unto them, Go ye into all the world, and preach the gospel to every creature. He that **believeth and is baptized shall be saved**; but he that believeth not shall be damned." - Mar 16:14-16 KJV*

*"Go ye therefore, and teach all nations, **baptizing them** in the name of the Father, and of the Son, and of the Holy Ghost: Teaching them to **observe all things whatsoever I have commanded you**: and, lo, I am with you always, even unto the end of the world. Amen." - Mat 28:19-20 KJV*

Many that day believed, repented, and were baptized which was a requirement for the salvation of the Jews. Jesus said, "He that believeth and is baptized shall be saved." There are two basic requirements stated in the previous Mark 16 and Matthew 28 passages.

1. Baptism is required for salvation.

2. Believers are to observe what Jesus commanded.

That is not the gospel of grace preached today. The current gospel is Paul's gospel found in 1 Corinthians 15:1-4.

*"Moreover, brethren, I declare unto you the gospel which I preached unto you, which also ye have received, and wherein ye stand; **By which also ye are saved**, if ye keep in memory what I preached unto you, unless ye have believed in vain. For I delivered unto you first of all that which I also received, how that **Christ died for our sins** according to the scriptures; And that he **was buried**, and that he **rose again the third day** according to the scriptures:" - 1Co 15:1-4 KJV*

This is a very simple gospel. I'm surprised so many can't seem to get this right. Most want to make it more complicated by adding some sort of works to the process thereby nullifying grace.

In Acts chapter 2:40-41, we read that many were saved that day.

*"And with many other words did he testify and exhort, saying, Save yourselves from this untoward generation. Then they that gladly received his word **were baptized**: and the same day there were added unto them about three thousand souls." - Act 2:40-41 KJV*

Untoward - perverse, troublesome; unmanageable, not easily guided or taught.

Three thousand Jews were baptized that day following Peter's instructions. Water baptism is not a requirement for salvation today. If you want to be baptized, that is fine, but it's not required. Notice the language here in verse 42. 3000 believers "were added unto them." Added unto who? If this were the beginning of the church, the body of Christ, the language would be different. But 3000 believers in Jesus as Messiah were added to an already existing group of believers, the "little flock" previously mentioned. These were Jews following Jesus their Messiah affectionately called by Jesus His "little flock." They were not Christians, as Christians did not exist until Acts chapter 13.

If you are not familiar with the term "little flock", let me take a minute to explain. This term, "little flock", was used by Jesus in Luke 12:32

*"Fear not, **little flock**; for it is your Father's good pleasure to give you the kingdom."*

Jesus was talking to those that followed Him during His earthly ministry. They were Jews that believed He was the promised Messiah to Israel. They believed the gospel of the kingdom that John the Baptist started preaching in Matthew chapter 3 and Jesus in Matthew chapter 4. Later the disciples went out preaching the same gospel of the kingdom. Here are a few versus to consider.

*"In those days came John the Baptist, preaching in the wilderness of Judaea, And saying, **Repent ye: for the kingdom of heaven is at hand**." - Mat 3:1-2 KJV*

*"From that time Jesus began to preach, and to say, **Repent: for the kingdom of heaven is at hand**." - Mat 4:17 KJV*

*"And Jesus went about all Galilee, teaching in their synagogues, and preaching the **gospel of the kingdom**, and healing all manner of sickness and all manner of disease among the people." - Mat 4:23 KJV*

*"These twelve Jesus sent forth, and commanded them, saying, Go not into the way of the Gentiles, and into any city of the Samaritans enter ye not: But go rather to the lost sheep of the house of Israel. And as ye go, preach, saying, **The kingdom of heaven is at hand**." - Mat 10:5-7 KJV*

The "little flock" are those of the lost sheep of the house of Israel, Jews, that believed in Jesus as Messiah. They were the believing remnant of the house of Israel. This believing remnant did not disappear at the crucifixion. They continued into the book of Acts. The 120 believers in the upper room in Acts chapter 1 were part of the "little flock." They were all Jews as we will read.

This "little flock" assembly of believers in their Messiah Jesus was the church, or assembly, that Jesus said He would build in Matthew chapter 16.

One last thing.

"And all that believed were together and had all things common; And sold their possessions and goods, and parted them to all men, as every man had need." - Act 2:44-45 KJV

Is this what happens today? Is this our model? When people get saved do they sell their possessions and join a Christian commune? No, not hardly. So why did those Jews do that back then? They were preparing for the 7-year Tribulation. They had a much better chance of enduring the wrath of God in a group than alone. Besides, this is the remnant that the Lord would protect during the Tribulation as defined in Revelation chapter 12 where the woman, Israel, will be protected for 3 ½ years, so they need to stay together.

This also harkens to Acts chapter 5 where Ananias and Sapphira sold some property and were to give the money to the group of believers at Jerusalem. However, they lied and kept some of the money. They were subsequently both killed by the Holy Spirit. Rejoice and be happy that we are not in that program.

So, did the church, the body of Christ begin in Acts chapter 2 as church tradition tells us, or was Peter preparing a remnant of Israel to enter the time of Jacob's trouble, the 7-year Tribulation, where God would try Israel by fire for their rejection of His Son, Jesus Christ. The answer is obvious to anyone that will simply study the scriptures.

Mat 3:11 KJV. John the Baptist speaking to Israel.

*"I indeed baptize you with water unto repentance: but he that cometh after me is mightier than I, whose shoes I am not worthy to bear: **he shall baptize you with the Holy Ghost, and with fire**:"*

The baptism of the Holy Spirit came to Israel at Pentecost in Acts chapter 2. The baptism of fire is the time of Jacob's trouble, the 7-year Tribulation which was to follow Acts chapter 2 had the rulers of Israel accepted Jesus as Israel's Messiah. But the Father intervened and instituted a program to save Gentiles, this present dispensation of Grace. The prophetic plan for Israel was placed on hold. It will resume after the Rapture of the church. Then all the prophecies about the Tribulation and the second coming of Christ will be fulfilled. There are 2 critical points of understanding about Acts chapter 2.

1st Critical point:

Peter is proclaiming the beginning of the "last days" for Israel, the 7-year Tribulation. That's why he quotes from the prophet Joel as Joel prophesied about the last days, the time of Jacob's trouble. Jacob's name was changed to Israel so it's the time of Israel's trouble.

2nd Critical point:

Peter is NOT proclaiming the beginning of the Church, the Body of Christ!

God gave Paul the revelation of the mystery doctrines concerning the dispensation of grace, the gospel of grace, and the body of Christ. Paul was not saved until Acts chapter 9 so anything occurring in the previous chapters could not pertain to us the body of Christ.

*"If ye have heard of the **dispensation of the grace of God** which is **given me** to you-ward: How that by **revelation** he made known unto me the mystery; (as I wrote afore in few words, Whereby, when ye read, ye may understand my knowledge in the **mystery of Christ**)" - Eph 3:2-4*

The revelation of this present church age was given to the apostle Paul after his conversion in Acts chapter 9. Therefore, the body of Christ could not have existed in Acts chapter 2.

Acts Chapter 3

The setting is still Jerusalem and the Temple. The chapter opens with Peter healing a lame man by the Temple.

*"Then Peter said, Silver and gold have I none; but such as I have give I thee: In the **name of Jesus Christ of Nazareth** rise up and walk. And he took him by the right hand, and lifted him up: and immediately his feet and ankle bones received strength. And he leaping up stood, and walked, and entered with them into the temple, walking, and leaping, and praising God." - Acts 3:6-8 KJV*

Peter will give an account of his actions in chapter 4. The chapter continues with Peter addressing the Jews.

*"And when Peter saw it, he answered unto the people, **Ye men of Israel**, why marvel ye at this? or why look ye so earnestly on us, as though by our own power or holiness we had made this man to walk?" - Acts 3:12.*

Peter addresses the men of Israel, not Gentiles. He uses this occasion to give his second sermon about Jesus, the Messiah of Israel.

*"The God of Abraham, and of Isaac, and of Jacob, the God of our fathers, hath **glorified his Son Jesus**; whom ye **delivered up**, and **denied** him in the presence of Pilate, when he was determined to let him go. But ye **denied the Holy One** and the Just, and desired a murderer to be granted unto you; And **killed the Prince of life**, whom God hath **raised from the dead**; whereof we are witnesses." - Acts 3:13-15 KJV*

Peter again chastises the Jews for killing their Messiah. He certainly is not preaching salvation via the death, burial, and resurrection of Jesus Christ, the gospel of grace.

*"Repent ye therefore, and be converted, that your sins may be blotted out, when the **times of refreshing** shall come from the presence of the Lord; And he shall send Jesus Christ, which before was preached unto you: Whom the heaven must receive until the **times of restitution of all things**,*

which God hath spoken by the mouth of all his holy prophets since the world began." - Acts 3:19–21 KJV

Peter instructs the Jews to repent that their sins may be forgiven or "blotted out." Their forgiveness comes, not when they repent, but at the "time of refreshing," the coming kingdom. Their salvation comes when the Lord appears and they are in His presence. This happened at the start of the Millennial Reign of Christ, the "times of restitution of all things".

Acts chapter 3 speaks of Abraham, Isaac, Jacob, Moses, Samuel, and the prophets, all things Jewish.

"Ye are the children of the prophets, and of the covenant which God made with our fathers, saying unto Abraham, And in thy seed shall all the kindreds of the earth be blessed." - Acts 3:25 KJV

Acts Chapter 4

The setting in chapter 4 has not changed. Peter and John are in Jerusalem near the Temple preaching the resurrection of Jesus Christ, the Messiah of Israel. Remember, the word Christ means the anointed one, the Messiah.

The priest and rulers are highly agitated with Peter and John's preaching and the healing of the lame man outside the Temple. Peter and John are called before the rulers and priests.

*"And Annas the high priest, and Caiaphas, and John, and Alexander, and as many as were of the kindred of the high priest, were **gathered together at Jerusalem**. And when they had set them in the midst, they asked, By what power, or by what name, have ye done this?" - Acts 4:6-7.*

The high priest commanded Peter and John not to preach in the name of Jesus in Jerusalem. The setting is still entirely Jewish. Peter takes the opportunity to preach to the priests.

*"Be it known unto you all, and to all the **people of Israel**, that by the name of Jesus Christ of Nazareth, **whom ye crucified**, whom God raised from the dead, even by him doth this man stand here before you whole. This is the stone which was set at nought of you builders, which is become the head of the corner. **Neither is there salvation in any other: for there is none other name under heaven given among men, whereby we must be saved**." - Acts 4:10–12 KJV*

Peter boldly reminds the rulers and people of Israel that they crucified their Messiah, but God raised Him from the dead. Peter then makes an astonishing statement. Salvation is only available through Jesus Christ; only in the name of Jesus can one be saved. Today we know and even take for granted that salvation comes only by faith in Jesus Christ. But put yourself back with Peter here in Acts chapter 4. Can you imagine the outrage in the minds of the rulers hearing Peter proclaim that the man they crucified, Jesus of Nazareth, has risen from the dead and His name becomes the only means of salvation? Reminds me of some familiar passages.

*"And it shall come to pass, that whosoever **shall call on the name of the LORD shall be delivered**: for in mount Zion and in Jerusalem shall be deliverance, as the LORD hath said, and in the remnant whom the LORD shall call." - Joel 2:32 KJV*

"And it shall come to pass, that whosoever shall call on the name of the Lord shall be saved." - Acts 2:21 KJV

*"For whosoever shall call upon the **name of the Lord shall be saved.**"* - Romans 10:13 KJV

The priests and rulers commanded Peter and John not to preach in the name of Jesus.

*"And they called them, and commanded them **not to speak at all nor teach in the name of Jesus**. But Peter and John answered and said unto them, Whether it be right in the sight of God to hearken unto you more than unto God, judge ye. For we cannot but speak the things which we have seen and heard."* - Acts 4:18-20 KJV

Peter and John continue their ministry to Israel, the Jews, as that is what they had "seen and heard" from Jesus Christ during His earthly ministry. Jesus and His disciples preaching to the Jews.

The word "Gentiles" appears once in chapter 4.

*"For of a truth against thy holy child Jesus, whom thou hast anointed, both Herod, and Pontius Pilate, with the **Gentiles**, and the people of Israel, were gathered together, For to do whatsoever thy hand and thy counsel determined before to be done."* - Acts 4:27-28 KJV

However, the word "Gentiles" is part of a list of those that plotted Jesus' death or took part in the crucifixion. Certainly not a list of those receiving the gospel of grace.

Lastly, in chapter 4 we see Jewish believers sharing possessions and having all things in common.

*"And the multitude of them that believed were of one heart and of one soul: neither said any of them that ought of the things which he possessed was his own; but they **had all things common.**"* - Acts 4:32 KJV

Why were the believers at Jerusalem sharing their possessions? Was this a model for a socialist system? Certainly not! They shared their goods and stayed together in preparation for the coming 7-year Tribulation as Peter announced in Acts chapter 2. They were living in the "last days." But what happened? The "last days" did not come. The promised kingdom did not come. The 7-year Tribulation remains yet future. Instead of receiving the promised kingdom, God's judgment befell Israel in 70 A.D. Their Temple was destroyed, Jerusalem ransacked, thousands murdered, and the remaining people scattered among other nations. "We" happened, the dispensation of grace. I will explain more in the Acts chapter 7 section.

Acts Chapter 5

The chapter opens with the account of Ananias and Saphira who pledged to give the proceeds from the sale of some property to the group of believers at Jerusalem. But they withheld some of the money and lied about the sale. Peter knew what Ananias had done.

*"But Peter said, Ananias, why hath Satan filled thine heart to **lie to the Holy Ghost**, and to keep back part of the price of the land? Whiles it remained, was it not thine own? and after it was sold, was it not in thine own power? why hast thou conceived this thing in thine heart? thou hast not*

*lied unto men, but unto God. And Ananias hearing these words **fell down, and gave up the ghost**: and great fear came on all them that heard these things. And the young men arose, wound him up, and carried him out, and buried him." - Acts 5:3–6 KJV*

For lying to the Holy Ghost, Ananias was smitten by the Holy Ghost falling dead at the apostle's feet. A short time later Saphira comes.

*"And Peter answered unto her, Tell me whether ye sold the land for so much? And she said, **Yea, for so much**. Then Peter said unto her, How is it that ye have agreed together to **tempt the Spirit of the Lord**? behold, the feet of them which have buried thy husband are at the door, and shall carry thee out. **Then fell she down straightway** at his feet, and yielded up the ghost: and the young men came in, and found her dead, and, carrying her forth, buried her by her husband." - Acts 5:8–10 KJV*

What is happening here? Is the Holy Spirit operating in grace or judgment? Judgment obviously. I included these events to show that the dispensation of grace was not yet present on earth. If it were, Ananias and Saphira would not have been killed by the Holy Spirit. In the dispensation of grace, the Holy Spirit indwells and seals believers. He does not kill them. Lying, as bad as that is, does not carry a death sentence in the body of Christ, the church. These believers in chapter 5 are part of the "little flock," Jewish believers that follow Jesus as Messiah of Israel.

"And great fear came upon all the church, and upon as many as heard these things." - Acts 5:11 KJV

The church, the "little flock," were full of fear at seeing two of their fellow believers struck dead by the Holy Spirit for lying. If this paradigm were in effect today we would not be under grace but under fear.

The word "church" is used again in verse eleven. But remember, the word church simply means an assembly or called out ones. It is not synonymous with us, the body of Christ. Most Christians assume that the word church refers to us, the body of Christ, the church in this present dispensation of grace. But that creates confusion and the misapplication of Scripture. They would then assume that Acts chapter 2 and chapter 5 apply to us today. But the church in these chapters is the "little flock" church, not the body of Christ church. If you do not make this distinction you will also be confused about the early chapters of Acts.

Chapter 5 continues with Peter and John doing many signs and wonders in Jerusalem at the Temple. So much so that the rulers put them in prison.

*"But the angel of the Lord by night **opened the prison doors**, and brought them forth, and said, Go, stand and **speak in the temple** to the people all the words of this life." - Acts 5:19–20 KJV*

Afterward, Peter makes the following proclamation.

*"The God of our fathers raised up Jesus, **whom ye slew and hanged on a tree**. Him hath God exalted with his right hand to be a Prince and a Saviour, for to **give repentance to Israel**, and forgiveness of sins." - Act s5:30-31.*

Peter proclaims the crucifixion of Jesus was for the repentance of Israel. Gentiles are not yet part of God's plan of salvation and certainly not on Peter's agenda. That will change in Acts chapter ten.

Acts Chapter 6

In verse 1 we find the use of a word that might cause some to believe there were Gentiles believers present at Jerusalem.

*"And in those days, when the number of the disciples was multiplied, there arose a murmuring of the **Grecians** against the Hebrews, because their widows were neglected in the daily ministration."* *- Acts 6:1 KJV*

In Strong's Concordance, the word "Grecians" is "used in the New Testament of Jews born in foreign lands and speaking Greek." It does not refer to Gentiles.

*"And the word of God increased; and the number of the disciples multiplied in **Jerusalem** greatly; and a great company of the **priests** were obedient to the faith. And Stephen, full of faith and power, did great wonders and miracles among the people."* *- Acts 6:7-8*

Those saved were Jews in Jerusalem, not Gentiles.

The disciples nominated Stephen to help with the distribution of goods and food specifically for the widows. But there arose a dispute between Stephen and other Jews.

*"Then there arose certain of the **synagogue**, which is called the **synagogue** of the Libertines, and Cyrenians, and Alexandrians, and of them of Cilicia and of Asia, disputing with Stephen."* *- Acts 6:9*

Those Jews from various synagogues accused Stephen of blasphemy against Moses.

"Then they suborned men, which said, We have heard him speak blasphemous words against Moses, and against God. And they stirred up the people, and the elders, and the scribes, and came upon him, and caught him, and brought him to the council, And set up false witnesses, which said, This man ceaseth not to speak blasphemous words against this holy place, and the law:" *- Acts 6:11-13*

All this in Jerusalem. The Jews framed Stephen and lied about him, setting him up for charges of blasphemy.

Acts Chapter 7

Stephen preaches to the council at Jerusalem beginning with Abraham, then the Exodus from Egypt, Moses giving the Law to Israel through Solomon and the First Temple.

*"Ye stiffnecked and uncircumcised in heart and ears, ye do always **resist the Holy Ghost: as your fathers did, so do ye**."* *- Acts 7:51.*

Stephen testified about Israel's continued rebellion against the Holy Ghost. For his message about Jesus, their Messiah, the Jews stoned him.

*"When they heard these things, they were **cut to the heart**, and they **gnashed on him with their teeth**. But he, being full of the Holy Ghost, looked up stedfastly into heaven, and saw the glory of God, and **Jesus standing on the right hand of God**, And said, Behold, I see the heavens opened, and the Son of man standing on the right hand of God. Then they cried out with a loud voice, and **stopped their ears**, and ran upon him with one accord, ... **And they stoned Stephen**, calling upon God, and saying, Lord Jesus, receive my spirit."* *- Acts 7:54-57, 59 KJV*

The extension of mercy from Pentecost to the stoning of Stephen gave Israel an additional year to repent and accept Jesus as their Messiah. But they did not. They rejected Stephen's message proclaiming Jesus as Israel's Messiah so violently that they killed him. Their judgment is clear "Cut it Down". The fall of Israel has begun.

Summary

The "Middle Wall of Partition" and the Law of Moses are in full force through Acts chapter 7. Those chapters are entirely Jewish with a focus on Jerusalem and the Temple. Therefore, the Body of Christ could not exist during the first seven chapters of Acts?

Did the church, the Body of Christ, really begin in Acts chapter 2 with the coming of the Holy Spirit? This is what we are told by most preachers, teachers, and scholars, but is it true?

The Body of Christ does not exist in the first seven chapters of Acts. The Apostle Paul is not saved until Acts chapter 9. No one in Acts chapters 1 through 7 has a ministry to take any gospel to the Gentiles. The "Middle Wall of Partition" is still present. Therefore, the Church, the Body of Christ cannot be present in Acts chapters 1-7 as there is no distinction in the Body of Christ between Jew and Gentile.

But doesn't Peter mention the church? Yes, he does. This is the assembly of Jewish believers, the "little flock," that have accepted Jesus as the Messiah of Israel. They are not the Body of Christ. I will discuss this in the next section.

Answers to the basic questions.

1. Who is speaking? The primary voice is the Holy Spirit speaking through the apostle Peter and the writer Luke.
2. Who is the intended audience? Israel, the Jews. Acts 1-7 is entirely Jewish; Jewish apostles, Jewish feast, Jews from the entire region hearing a Jewish gospel.
3. What is the timeframe or the setting? Post ascension, the giving of the Holy Spirit, the assembly of Jews believing in Messiah Jesus mostly in Jerusalem by the Temple.

Chapter Six – But Now, The Church Age

The "But Now" section, the Church Age, the Dispensation of Grace, this present period wherein God is saving Gentiles, properly named the Body of Christ.

First, the word "church":

- The Greek word for "church" is *ekklēsia*. It means called out ones or assembly.
- *Ekklēsia*, used over 300 times in the Septuagint, refers to an assembly of Jews at the Synagogue. The Septuagint is a Greek translation of the Old Testament written around 270 B.C.
- "Church" can mean an assembly of Christians.
- "Church" can also mean any assembly of Jews.
- Stephen, in Acts chapter 7 refers to Israel after the exodus from Egypt as a church.

*"This is he, that was in the **church in the wilderness** with the angel which spake to him in the mount Sinai, and with our fathers: who received the lively oracles to give unto us:" – Acts 7:38*

Do not be confused by the word "church". It must be understood within the context of the passage wherein it is used. It does not always refer to the Body of Christ in the dispensation of grace.

In Hebrews, we read the following about the church.

*"Saying, I will declare thy name unto my brethren, in the midst of the **church** will I sing praise unto thee." – Hebrews 2:12*

One would naturally assume this "church" to be the Body of Christ. But this is a quote from Psalm 22.

*"I will declare thy name unto my brethren: in the midst of the **congregation** will I praise thee." – Psalm 22:22*

In the Old Testament, an assembly of Jews was called a congregation. The word congregation was used 333 times in the Old Testament. It means the same as the word church used in the New Testament. Do not be fooled by the word church. It is not synonymous with the Body of Christ. In the Hebrew epistles, Hebrews thru Revelation, church means a body of Jewish believers following their Messiah, Jesus Christ. See the Little Flock section.

Continuing with the "But Now" section, the Dispensation of Grace, the current program God has implemented to save Gentiles. We will answer the following questions.

1. Is the "Middle Wall of Partition" still present?
2. Is the Law of Moses still in effect?
3. Why is it labeled a "Mystery"?
4. Is this period a continuation of something from the Old Testament or something new?
5. What is so special about the apostle Paul?
6. When did the Body of Christ begin?

Church in the Wilderness	Church Jesus will Build	Church at Jerusalem	Church, the Body of Christ
"This is he, that was in the church in the wilderness with the angel which spake to him in the mount Sinai," - Act 7:38	"And I say also unto thee, That thou art Peter, and upon this rock I will build my church," - Mat 16:18	"Praising God, and having favour with all the people. And the Lord added to the church daily such as should be saved." - Act 2:47	"Now ye are the body of Christ, and members in particular." - 1Co 12:27 "And hath put all [things] under his feet and gave him [to be] the head over all [things] to the church, Which is his body, the fulness of him that filleth all in all." - Eph 1:22-23
Moses	Jesus	Peter	Paul
Old Testament Church	New Testament Church	New Testament Church	Body of Christ Church
Prophecy	Prophecy	Prophecy	Mystery

Table 1 - Churches

Let's discuss the "Mystery" aspect first. The following two passages of scripture declare the **prophetic** nature of Jesus' first coming.

*"Blessed be the Lord God of Israel; for he hath visited and redeemed his people, And hath raised up an horn of salvation for us in the house of his servant David; As he **spake by the mouth of his holy prophets, which have been since the world began**:" - Luke 1:68–70*

*"And he shall send Jesus Christ, which before was preached unto you: Whom the heaven must receive until the times of restitution of all things, **which God hath spoken by the mouth of all his holy prophets since the world began**." - Acts 3:20–21*

The prophecy about the redemption of Israel "was spoken by the mouth of the prophets since the world began." Therefore, it was not a mystery but a well-known prophecy.

It is also clear that the ministry and redemptive purposes of Jesus were matters of prophecy "spoken by the mouth of the prophets since the world began." This also is not a mystery.

But the apostle Paul spoke the following about the gospel of grace.

*"Now to him that is of power to stablish you according to my gospel, and the preaching of Jesus Christ, according to the **revelation of the mystery, which was kept secret since the world began**," - Romans 16:25*

The gospel of grace given to the apostle Paul by revelation was a "mystery" that had been "kept secret since the world began." The "Mystery" of the gospel of grace was unknown to Old Testament prophets, unknown to Jesus' disciples, unknown to anyone before it was revealed to the apostle Paul beginning in Acts chapter 9.

Another important passage that reveals the mystery aspect of the church, the Body of Christ:

*"Unto me, who am less than the least of all saints, is this grace given, that I should preach among the Gentiles the **unsearchable riches of Christ**; And to make all men see what is the **fellowship of the mystery**, which from the **beginning of the world hath been hid in God**, who created all things by Jesus Christ:" – Ephesians 3:8-9*

A couple of points here.

1. The doctrines and gospel of grace were given to the apostle Paul, not Peter, James, or John.
2. Only Paul had a ministry to the Gentiles in the Book of Acts.
3. The gospel of grace was a "mystery" before revealed to the apostle Paul.
4. This mystery was "hid in God" from the beginning of the world. It was not hidden in the Old Testament.

Could the Holy Spirit make this any clearer? The church, the Body of Christ, the dispensation of grace was completely unknown to anyone before the apostle Paul, it was "hid in God".

This is a **critical understanding** because it reveals the uniqueness of the church, the Body of Christ. The church is not a continuation of something from the Old Testament or the gospels. It is a brand-new entity else it would not be a mystery.

Let's take a fresh look at the "But now" passage from Ephesians chapter 2.

*"**But now** in Christ Jesus ye who sometimes were far off are made nigh by the blood of Christ. For he is our peace, who hath **made both one**, and hath **broken down the middle wall of partition** between us; Having **abolished** in his flesh the **enmity**, even the **law of commandments** contained in ordinances; for to make in himself of **twain one new man**, so making peace;" – Ephesians 2:13-15*

*   "But Now" – This refers to the present dispensation of grace that began with the apostle Paul and will end at the Rapture.
*   "made both one" – there is no difference between Jew and Gentile in the Body of Christ.
*   "broken down the middle wall of partition" – the wall of partition that separated Jew from Gentile has been broken down by Jesus Christ.
*   "enmity" - Jesus has abolished the enmity between Jew and Gentile.
*   "law of commandments" – Jesus has also abolished the law of Moses as it pertains to the Body of Christ. Since there is no difference between Jew and Gentile, the Law of Moses cannot be in effect.
*   "twain, one new man" – the twain, Jew, and Gentile are now one new man in Christ. We are not a continuation of Old Testament believers. We are not a continuation of believers during the ministry of Jesus Christ or the early chapters of Acts. We are a completely NEW man, the Body of Christ, that began with the apostle Paul.

Mystery Program

Since the church, the Body of Christ, was a mystery, let's look at some of the mystery passages.

*   The mystery of blindness to Israel during the Church age (Romans 11:25)

- The revelation of the Mystery of the gospel of grace given to Paul (Rom 16:25)
- Mystery Hidden wisdom of God that Grace would come to the Gentiles (1Co 2:7-8)
- The mystery of the Rapture of the Church (1Co 15:51-52)
- The mystery of all things in Christ in heaven and earth (Eph 1:9-10)
- The mystery of the Dispensation of Grace given to Paul (Eph 3:1-4)
- The mystery that Gentiles are fellow heirs with Israel (Eph 3:5-7)
- The mystery of Grace Hid in God (Eph 3:9)
- The Mystery members of His Body (Eph 5:30, 32)
- The mystery of the Gospel of Grace (Eph 6:19)
- The mystery of Christ in you the hope of glory (Col 1:26-27)

Now you can easily see why Paul commands us to "Rightly Divide the Word of Truth". Because the Body of Christ is unique. It is completely different from what came before it and what will come after it. Most pastors and teachers want to harmonize the scriptures (the Old Testament, the Gospels, the book of Acts, Paul's epistles, and Hebrews through Revelation). However, Paul commands us to rightly divide the word based upon God's interaction with mankind and His designated audience.

Clearly, from our study thus far, God's designated audience in the Old Testament, the Gospels, and Acts chapters 1-7 was Israel, His chosen people, the Jews.

Only after the saving of Saul of Tarsus on the road to Damascus, does God's program begin to change. Now God includes Gentiles in His plan of redemption. God chose Saul, the apostle Paul, to reveal His new program to save Gentiles, and that program is ongoing. That program is the Dispensation of Grace.

Why the Big Mystery?

The entire dispensation of grace was a mystery hid in God. But why was it a mystery? Why was it not part of Bible prophecy? Well, God had an exceptionally good reason for the mystery and here it is.

*"But we speak the wisdom of God in **a mystery**, even the **hidden wisdom**, which God ordained **before the world** unto our glory: Which **none of the princes of this world knew**: for had they known it, **they would not have crucified the Lord of glory**." - 1 Corinthians 2:7-8*

This is an immensely powerful verse that you must understand and understand correctly. The dispensation of grace, God's program to save Gentiles, was hidden in God the Father from "before the world" began. None of the "princes of this world knew" this hidden wisdom. The "princes of this world" is not a reference to leaders and rulers like King Herod, Pontius Pilate, or the high priest. It is a reference to princes in the spiritual realm; demons, fallen angels, and Satan himself. They did not know the "hidden wisdom" held in the power of the Father.

The verse goes on to say that had the princes of this world known the "hidden wisdom" they would not have crucified the Lord Jesus Christ. Pagan Gentiles had been Satan's possession since the fall of Adam in the garden. They had been in Satan's back pocket for millennia. But now, during the dispensation of grace, untold millions of Gentiles have been saved by simple faith in the blood of Jesus Christ as payment for sin. Had Satan known that through the crucifixion of Jesus Christ millions of Gentiles would be saved, he would have done everything possible to prevent the crucifixion of Jesus. But, not knowing the hidden wisdom, Satan worked tirelessly to ensure the death of Jesus on the cross. Even to the point of possessing Judas Iscariot to ensure the job was done right. Are you beginning to understand the uniqueness of the dispensation of grace, the gospel of grace, and the body of Christ?

Chapter Seven - The Fall of Israel

Romans chapter 11 solidifies the starting point of the dispensation of grace.

*"I say then, Have **they stumbled** that they should **fall**? God forbid: but rather through their fall **salvation is come unto the Gentiles**, for to provoke them to jealousy. Now if the fall of them be the riches of the world, and the **diminishing** of them the riches of the Gentiles; how much more their fulness?" - Romans 11:11-12*

Paul is asking the question, has Israel stumbled that they should fall? When did Israel stumble? They stumbled at the crucifixion of Jesus.

*"But we preach **Christ crucified**, unto the Jews a **stumblingblock**, and unto the Greeks foolishness;" – 1ˢᵗ Corinthians 1:23*

If the Jews stumbled at the cross, when did they fall? As we read in Acts chapter 7, Israel fell with the stoning of Stephen by rejecting their final offer to accept Jesus as their Messiah. They were given a one-year extension of mercy. But their rejection of Stephen's testimony of Christ, caused Israel to be cut down, they fell. But by their fall, salvation comes to the Gentiles. The progression is clear; the Jews must reject Jesus as Messiah and then salvation would come to the Gentiles.

1. Israel stumbled at the cross of Christ.
2. They fell at the stoning of Stephen.
3. Following that, salvation came to the Gentiles.

The preceding passage from Romans chapter 11 establishes the division between the "Time Past" and "But Now" periods. The division event is the fall of Israel in Acts chapter 7. Jesus saves the apostle Paul In Acts chapter 9 beginning the dispensation of Grace. The book of Acts records the diminishing of Israel and the growth of the dispensation of grace. A transition moving away from Israel, Jerusalem, the Temple, Peter, and the Law of Moses, to the Gentiles, Antioch, the apostle Paul, and grace.

The apostle Paul is the apostle to the dispensation of Grace, the Body of Christ, this present church age.

*"For I speak to you Gentiles, inasmuch as **I am the apostle of the Gentiles**, I magnify mine office:" - Romans 11:13*

*"Whereunto I am ordained a preacher, and an apostle, (I speak the truth in Christ, and lie not;) **a teacher of the Gentiles** in faith and verity." – 1ˢᵗ Timothy 2:7*

*"Whereunto I am appointed a preacher, and an apostle, and a **teacher of the Gentiles**." – 2ⁿᵈ Timothy 1:11*

The writings of the apostle Paul are exclusive to the church, the Body of Christ, which is primarily a Gentile assembly of believers. Paul's epistles are for this current dispensation of grace.

Let's answer the questions I asked at the beginning of the "But Now" section, Romans through Philemon.

1. Is the "Middle Wall of Partition" between Jew and Gentile still present? No, the middle wall of partition was broken down by Jesus and there is no distinction between Jew and Gentile (Eph. 2:14) in this present dispensation of grace.
2. Is the Law of Moses still in effect? No, the law has been abolished for the Body of Christ. We are not under the Law as Gentiles were never under the Law of Moses (Eph. 2:15).
3. Why is it labeled a "Mystery"? The dispensation of grace was hidden in God and kept secret from the beginning of the world. It was a secret plan to save Gentiles and bring them to Christ (Eph. 3:9).
4. Is the dispensation of grace a continuation of something from the Old Testament or something new? Something new, we are one new man, the Body of Christ (Eph. 2:15).
5. What is so special about the apostle Paul? The apostle Paul is the first and only person ever called by God into a ministry to Gentiles (Eph. 3:8).
6. When did the Body of Christ begin? The Body of Christ technically began with the saving of the apostle Paul on the road to Damascus. He was the first member of the one new man (1 Tim. 1:16).

In Chart 7 please notice the following.

- The "Time Past" section pertains to "Prophecy".
  ✓ Much in the Old Testament pertains to prophecy about Israel
  ✓ The birth, ministry, and death of Jesus Christ are in Old Testament prophecy

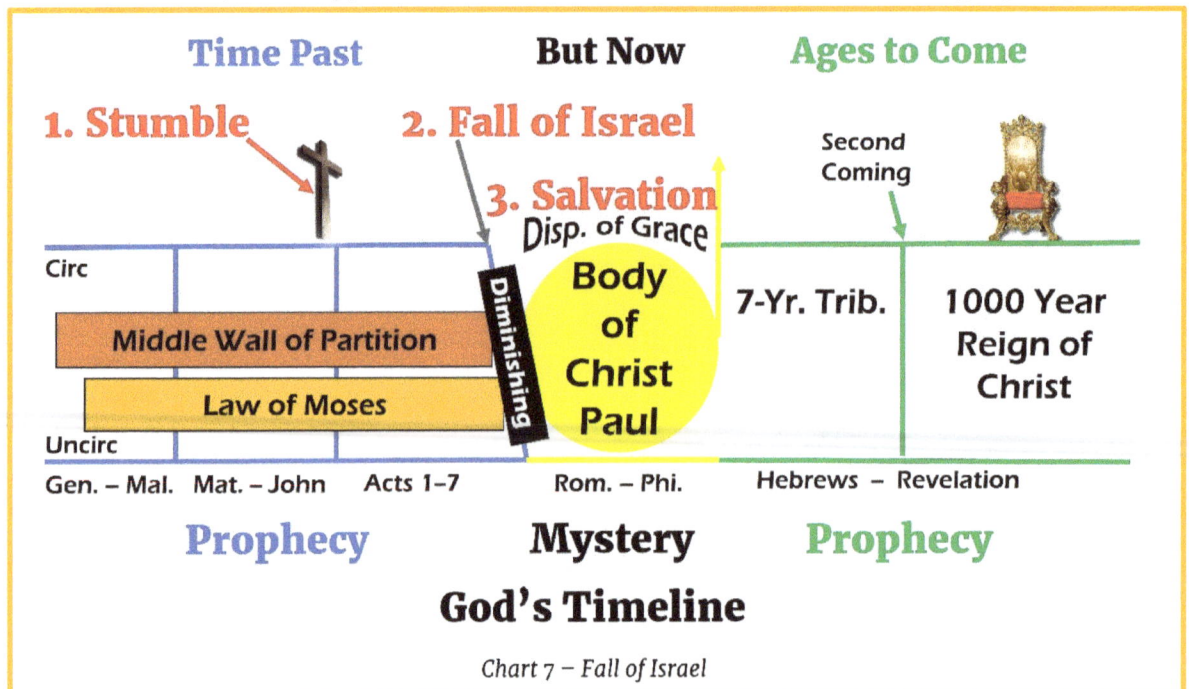

Chart 7 – Fall of Israel

- ✓ In Acts chapter 2 Peter quotes the prophecy of Joel.
- The "But Now" section pertains to "Mystery".
  - ✓ The dispensation of grace was a mystery hid in God, kept secret from the beginning of the world
  - ✓ The Body of Christ, the gospel of grace, the one new man, the rapture, all a secret hid in God.
- The "Ages to Come" section pertains to "Prophecy".
  - ✓ The 7-year Tribulation, the 70th week of Daniels prophecy, a prophecy.
  - ✓ The coming Antichrist, a prophecy.
  - ✓ The second coming of Jesus Christ at the end of the 7-year Tribulation is a prophecy.
  - ✓ The salvation of Israel at that time is a prophecy.
  - ✓ The kingdom of the Messiah, prophecy.

As you can see, anything dealing with "Prophecy" is for Israel including their Messiah Jesus Christ. Things dealing with the Church, the Body of Christ, are a mystery. Therefore, the Church is not part of Old Testament prophecy and cannot exist in the gospels or Acts before chapter 9. The church cannot exist in the 7-year Tribulation as that is a prophecy about Israel. All Old Testament prophecy pertains to Israel. Mystery pertains to the Church, the Body of Christ. Do not mix the two as that only leads to confusion.

Let's answer our three basic right division questions.

1. Who is speaking? The primary voice in Romans thru Philemon is the Holy Spirit speaking through the apostle Paul.
2. Who is the intended audience? The Body of Christ, true believers in the atoning death, burial, and resurrection of Jesus Christ.
3. What is the timeframe or the setting? The Gentile church age beginning with the saving of Saul (Paul) and closing with the Rapture of the church.

Chapter Eight – The Little Flock Explained

The Dispensation of Grace begins in Acts chapter 9 with the Lord Jesus arresting Saul of Tarsus on the road to Damascus. The Lord saved Saul giving him the revelation of grace (Galatians 1:11-12). The Dispensation of Grace begins, and Paul (Saul) is the first to preach the gospel of grace focused on the atoning death, burial, and resurrection of Jesus Christ. This begins the Body of Christ, this present church age of grace. But what about those who believed in Jesus during His earthly ministry and the thousands saved in the early chapters of Acts? Many were saved before Paul's ministry started. What were they? They were the church before the church.

In Luke chapter 12, Jesus speaks to Jews that believe and follow Him as the Messiah. He was preparing them for the Kingdom He offered to Israel. Remember, John the Baptist, Jesus and the 12 disciples preached the gospel of the kingdom. At that time no one knew of the dispensation of grace as it was still a mystery hid in God.

"And seek not ye what ye shall eat, or what ye shall drink, neither be ye of doubtful mind. For all these things do the nations of the world seek after: and your Father knoweth that ye have need of these things. But rather seek ye the **kingdom of God***; and all these things shall be added unto you."* – Luke 12:29-31

"Fear not, **little flock***; for it is your Father's good pleasure to give you the* **kingdom***. Sell that ye have, and give alms; provide yourselves bags which wax not old, a treasure in the heavens that faileth not, where no thief approacheth, neither moth corrupteth. For where your treasure is, there will your heart be also."* – Luke 12:32-34

Jesus called those Jews that believed and followed Him by the endearing name "little flock." How fitting as they were the believing remnant of the "lost sheep of the house of Israel." This group of Jews believed in Jesus as the Messiah of Israel. They began during the ministry of John the Baptist and continued into the early chapters of Acts. After Acts chapter 9 they diminished as the Dispensation of Grace expanded.

But didn't Jesus talk about building His church? Was He talking about us, the Body of Christ? Let's look at the passage.

"And Simon Peter answered and said, **Thou art the Christ, the Son of the living God***. ... And I say also unto thee, That thou art Peter, and upon this rock I will build my* **church***; and the gates of hell shall not prevail against it."* – Matthew 16:16, 18

Jesus stated He would build His church upon the rock of Him being the "Christ", the "Son of God." The word "Christ" is the English translation of the Greek word *Christos* meaning, the anointed one, the Messiah. What church or assembly was built on the belief that Jesus was the Messiah? The "little flock" church of Jews was saved during Jesus' earthly ministry and in the early chapters of Acts. They followed Jesus as Messiah and they were all Jews.

Also, Jesus was speaking to Peter and Peter was the head of the Jewish church in Jerusalem. We, the Body of Christ assembly of believers, mostly Gentiles, are not saved by believing Jesus is the Messiah of Israel. Our salvation comes by believing in the atoning death of Jesus on the cross, His burial, and His resurrection on the third day (1 Cor. 15:1-4). There are two separate churches during the book of Acts transition period. One of the Jews following their Messiah Jesus. The other following Paul and the gospel of grace. The "little flock" and the "body of Christ."

Continuing in Matthew chapter 16 we read:

"From that time forth began Jesus to shew unto his disciples, how that he must go unto **Jerusalem***, and* **suffer many things** *of the elders and chief priests and scribes,* **and be killed***, and be raised again the third day. Then Peter took him, and began to* **rebuke him***, saying, Be it far from thee, Lord: this shall not be unto thee. But he turned, and said unto Peter, Get thee behind me, Satan: thou art an offence unto me: for thou savourest not the things that be of God, but those that be of men."* – Matthew 16:21-23

Jesus announced that He must go to Jerusalem, be killed, then rise from the dead on the third day. Peter rebuked Jesus for this statement, making it clear that he does not yet understand the redemption Jesus will secure for mankind on the cross. Peter also knew nothing of the dispensation of grace later revealed to Paul. The early believers in Messiah Jesus were the "little flock", not the body of Christ.

Jesus' proclamation about His "church" in Matthew chapter 16 is not the Body of Christ but the assembly of Jews believing Jesus is their Messiah. This assembly of Jews began during Jesus' ministry and continued into the early chapters of Acts. This is the church that officially began in Acts chapter 2 with the coming of the Holy Spirit. The contrast between the early believers in Jesus as Messiah and the later Body of Christ that believed in Jesus as Lord and Savior is clear. Remember, Gentiles were never promised a Messiah, only Israel.

The last verse in Acts chapter 2 states that souls were saved that day and added to the church. Is this the Body of Christ?

"Praising God, and having favour with all the people. And the Lord added to the church daily such as should be saved." – Acts 2:47

Those saved in Acts chapter 2 on the day of Pentecost were all Jews as we have seen. They responded to Peter's preaching wherein he criticized Israel for crucifying their Messiah. The gospel Peter preached was the gospel given to the disciples in Mark 16:14-18. Repent and be baptized is the gospel Peter preached. He did not preach the gospel of grace later given to Paul for the Gentiles. The "church" the Lord added to that day was the "little flock."

A comparison of the "little flock" with the body of Christ reveals they are not synonymous but two distinct groups of believers in Jesus Christ, one as Messiah, the other as Lord and Savior.

Scripture Passage:
        Little flock – Luke 12:29-31
        Body of Christ – 1st Corinthians 12:27 & Ephesians 1:22-23
Speakers:
        Little flock – Jesus, Peter, James, John, and the disciples.
        Body of Christ – Paul
Gospel Message:

	Little Flock	**Body of Christ**
Scripture passage	Luke 12:29-31	1 Cor 12:27 & Ephesians 1:22-23
Speakers	Jesus, Peter and the apostles	Paul
Gospel message	Believe and be baptized - Mark 16:14-18	Gospel of Grace - 1 Cor 15:1-4
Audience	Jews & proselytes	Jews & Gentiles
Model	Law keeping churches	Grace churches
Center	Jerusalem -Acts Ch. 1-7	Antioch Acts Ch. 13
Operation	Diminish during Acts - Rom 11:11-12	Expand during Acts
Current	No, the Little Flock existed only during Jesus ministry and the book of Acts.	Began in Acts 9 with the saving of Saul and continues to the Rapture of the Body of Christ

Chart 9 – Little Flock, BOC

Little flock – Believe and be baptized, Mark 16:14-18
Body of Christ – Grace through faith, 1st Cor 15:1-4

Audience:
Little flock – Jews and proselytes.
Body of Christ – Jews and Gentiles, mostly Gentiles.

Model:
Little flock – Law-keeping churches or assemblies.
Body of Christ – Grace churches.

Center:
Little flock – Jerusalem, Acts chapters 1-7
Body of Christ – Antioch, Acts chapter 13

Operation:
Little flock – Diminish during Acts – Rom 11:11-12
Body of Christ – Expand and grow during Acts.

Current state:
Little flock – The Little Flock existed only during the ministry of Jesus and the book of Acts.
Body of Christ – Began in Acts chapter 9 with the saving of Saul, our apostle Paul, and continues to the Rapture of the church.

You must understand the two churches existing in the time period of the book of Acts. Acts is a transitional book moving from the "little flock" of Jews following their Messiah to the Body of Christ following the gospel of grace, the death, burial, and resurrection of Jesus Christ.

In Paul's greeting to the saints at Corinth we find an interesting passage ignored by most Christians because they have no clue about the dichotomy of the "little flock" and the Body of Christ.

*"Paul, called to be an apostle of Jesus Christ through the will of God, and Sosthenes our brother, Unto the church of God which is at Corinth, to them that are sanctified in Christ Jesus, called to be saints, with all that in every place call upon the name of Jesus Christ our Lord, **both theirs and ours**:" - 1Cor 1:1-2*

Paul identifies himself as the author and opens with a standard greeting to the saints. The passage is clear and concise until the phrase "both theirs and ours." What does Paul mean by "theirs and ours?"

In Corinth, there were Jews that believed in Jesus the Messiah. They were part of the "little flock." There were also Greeks that believed the gospel of grace placing them into the Body of Christ. The phrase "Theirs and ours" addresses the "little flock" and the Body of Christ coexisting during the time period of Acts. The transition from "little flock" to the Body of Christ is shown in Chart 8.

Both groups are churches. Both groups are saved and filled with the Holy Spirit. Both groups worship God through Jesus Christ. But each has a different gospel message as listed in Chart 9. For the Jew, the good news is to believe in Jesus the Messiah and be baptized. For the Gentile the good news is to believe in the atoning death, burial, and resurrection of Jesus Christ; no baptism is required. Two different gospels, both pointing to Jesus Christ as Savior, both giving the Holy Spirit to believers.

We've learned that Paul's epistles were written to the Body of Christ. But what about the epistles of Peter, James, and John? To whom were those books written? To answer this question let's continue with the "Ages to Come" period.

Chapter Nine - Ages to Come

Is the "Middle Wall of Partition" and the Law of Moses in operation during the 7-year Tribulation and the Millennial reign of Jesus Christ? Galatians chapter 2 holds some important scriptures that demand our attention. Paul, writing to the Body of Christ in Galatia, recounts his visit to Jerusalem 14 years after his conversion. Here we will learn the intended audience for the writings of Peter, James and John, commonly called the Hebrew Epistles.

*"But contrariwise, when they saw that the **gospel of the uncircumcision** was committed unto **me**, as the gospel of the **circumcision was unto Peter**; (For he that wrought effectually in **Peter to the apostleship of the circumcision**, the same was mighty in **me toward the Gentiles**:)" - Galatians 2:7-8*

Four points must be understood from this passage.

1. The gospel of the uncircumcision, Gentiles, was committed to the apostle Paul.
2. The gospel of the circumcision, Israel, was committed to the apostle Peter.
3. Peter was an apostle to the circumcision, Israel.
4. Paul was the apostle to the Gentiles.

This passage might seem confusing. That is why you have never heard a sermon on it. But it is very straight forward when taken literally and rightly divided. Jesus commanded Peter and the other apostles in Mark 16:14-18 to preach the gospel of "believe and be baptized". They had to believe Jesus was their Messiah for salvation. This gospel was obviously for the Jews, the "little flock." It is the "gospel of the circumcision." Peter preached this gospel at Pentecost in Acts chapter 2 to an audience entirely Jewish. Peter was an apostle to the Jews.

Jesus Christ gave the gospel of grace to the apostle Paul by direct revelation; the gospel of the uncircumcision preached to Gentiles. Paul's gospel centers on the atoning death of Jesus, his burial, and resurrection on the third day (1 Cor 15:1-4). Paul was the apostle to the Gentiles.

In the book of Acts, two gospels are being preached.

1. The gospel preached by Peter and the other apostles to the Jews, the "little flock", following Jesus' instructions in Mark 16:14-18.
2. The gospel preached by Paul to the Gentiles, the gospel of grace.

The dual gospel pattern continues.

*"And when **James, Cephas, and John**, who seemed to be pillars, perceived the grace that was given unto **me**, they gave to me and Barnabas the right hands of fellowship; that **we should go unto the heathen**, and **they unto the circumcision**." - Galatians 2:9*

Verse 9 restates the pattern.

1. James, Cephas (Peter), and John are apostles to the circumcision, Israel.
2. Paul and Barnabas would go to the heathen, Gentiles.

So, here is the point. If James, Peter, and John were apostles to the Jews, who might you think would be the intended audience of their writings? Would they be writing to Gentiles or Jews? Jews, of course, as they are apostles to the Jews.

Paul, on the other hand, was the apostle to the Gentiles. Who was his intended audience, Jew or Gentile? Gentile, of course. Jesus spoke this to Ananias in Acts chapter 9 shortly after Saul's Damascus road conversion.

*"But the Lord said unto him, Go thy way: for he is a chosen vessel unto me, **to bear my name before the Gentiles**, and kings, and the children of Israel:" – Acts 9:15*

*"For I speak to you Gentiles, inasmuch as **I am the apostle of the Gentiles**, I magnify mine office:" – Romans 11:13*

Paul's epistles are Romans thru Philemon, written exclusively to the Body of Christ which is primarily Gentile. After Philemon comes the Hebrew epistles of Hebrews thru Revelation. These include the epistles of James, Peter, and John. Notice the Bible books of James, Peter and John are in the same order as Galatians 2:9, "James, Cephas, and John." Coincidence, hardly. God does not do coincidence. The books of Hebrews thru Revelation, written to Israel, are to guide them through the 7-year Tribulation where the Law of Moses is operational once again. When you read Hebrews thru Revelation read with the mindset of a Jew going through the 7-year Tribulation.

Book of Hebrews

The title of the book of Hebrews confirms the intended audience is Hebrews, Jews. I've heard many pastors, teachers, and tv preachers claim Hebrews was written to Hebrew Christians. This is nothing but bogus church tradition. There is no such creature as a Hebrew Christian for in the body of Christ there is no difference nor distinction between Jew and Gentile. For that reason, there would never be a book of the Bible written exclusively to Hebrew Christians. What about Gentile Christians? I guess the book of Hebrews would not apply to them, right? If you simply think it through, the concept of a Hebrew Christian quickly becomes ridiculous.

Let's look at some passages that confirm the intended audience is entirely Jewish and not the church.

*"God, who at sundry times and in divers manners spake in **time past** unto the **fathers** by the **prophets**, Hath in these **last days** spoken unto **us** by his Son, whom he hath appointed heir of all things, by whom also he made the worlds;" – Hebrews 1:1-2*

God spoke in "time past", the Old Testament, to the Fathers of Israel through the prophets. The prophets spoke prophecy to Israel, not Gentile nations. In the "last days" spoken to "us", Hebrews/Israel, by His Son. When did Jesus speak to Israel? He spoke to them during his 3-year earthly ministry. The first verse of Hebrews removes the reader from the

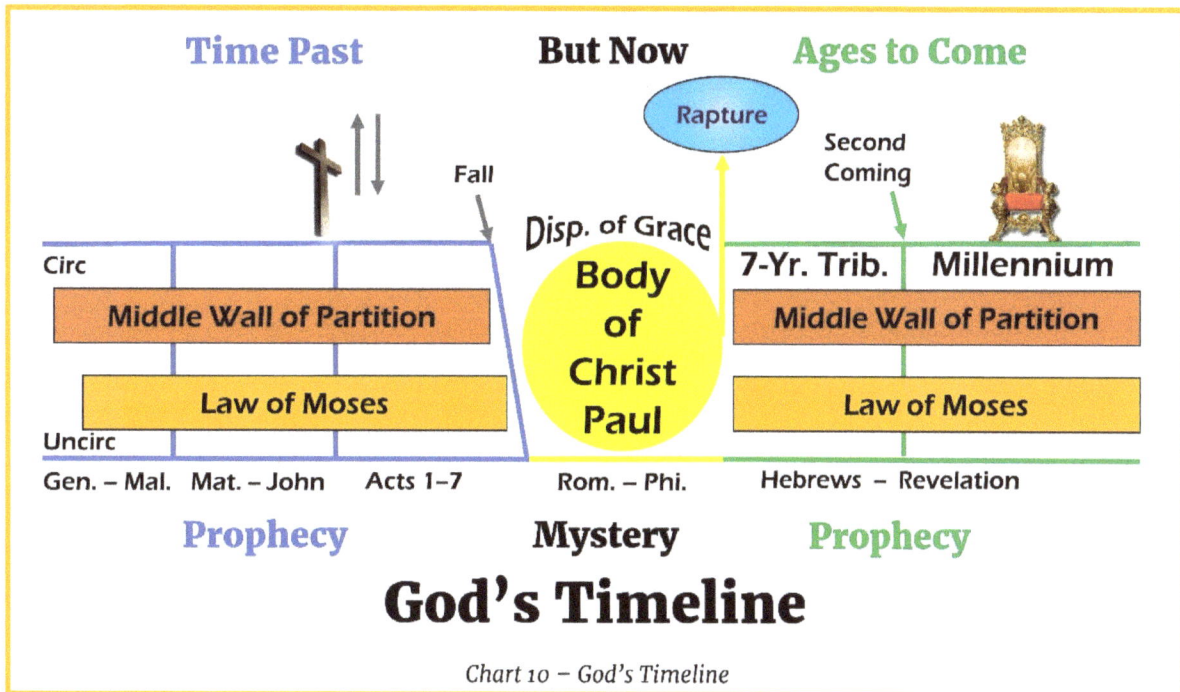

Chart 10 – God's Timeline

"Mystery" program of Paul back to the "Prophecy" program for Israel. The program has changed. The writer of Hebrews continues the "last days" theme from Jesus. Peter, James, and John.

*"How shall we **escape**, if we neglect so **great salvation**; which at the **first began to be spoken by the Lord**, and was **confirmed unto us by them that heard** him; God also bearing them witness, both with **signs and wonders**, and with divers miracles, and gifts of the Holy Ghost, according to his own will?"* – Hebrews 2:3-4

How shall the Jews "escape" the wrath of God if they neglect so "great salvation"? Well, they won't. This salvation was "first began to be spoken by the Lord" to Israel. Jesus spoke to Israel proclaiming himself their Messiah, the coming kingdom, and the imminent 7-yer Tribulation as recorded in Matthew chapters 24 and 25. The ministry of Jesus was validated by many "signs and wonders". We in the Body of Christ are not saved by the gospel spoken by Jesus Christ as that gospel was for the Jews. Those Jewish gospels were:

1. "Repent ye, for the kingdom of heaven is at hand" Matthew 3:2.

2. "He that believeth and is baptized shall be saved" Mark 16:16. We, in the church, are saved by the gospel of grace given to us by our apostle Paul (1 Cor 15:1-4). Hebrews 2:3-4 is for Israel as is the entire book.

Chapter 3 of Hebrews warns Israel not to harden their hearts as their fathers did in the wilderness after the Exodus. But to hold fast the confidence and the rejoicing of hope in

Christ firm unto the end (Heb 3:6). Jews must hold hope until the end of the 7-year Tribulation to receive salvation. We, the Body of Christ, have the assurance of salvation when we believe.

*"For we are made partakers of Christ, if we **hold the beginning of our confidence steadfast unto the end**;" - Hebrews 3:14*

The writer of Hebrews states that to be "made partakers of Christ", or saved, they must hold their confidence in Christ unto the end. The end of what? The end of the 7-year Tribulation. Jesus said the same in the book of Matthew.

*"And ye shall be hated of all men for my name's sake: but he that **endureth to the end shall be saved**." - Matthew 10:22*

*"But he that shall **endure unto the end**, the same shall be saved." - Matthew 24:13*

These passages are not about enduring to the end of your life, but the end of the Tribulation.

In Hebrews chapter 6 we read the following:

*"For it is **impossible** for those who were once enlightened, and have tasted of the heavenly gift, and were made partakers of the Holy Ghost, And have tasted the good word of God, and the powers of the world to come, **If they shall fall away, to renew them again unto repentance**; seeing they crucify to themselves the Son of God afresh, and put him to an open shame." - Hebrews 6:4-6*

Christians get into trouble and confusion trying to apply these passages in Hebrews to the Body of Christ. The above passage is for Israel only. If a Jew "falls away" from believing that Jesus is the Messiah during the 7-year Tribulation, it is impossible to "renew them again to repentance." A Jew could easily fall away by taking the mark of the beast. Anyone taking the mark of the beast is damned. There is no repentance or renewal available for them.

If a Christian backslides and falls away from Jesus Christ in this present dispensation of grace, he can repent and return to fellowship with Christ. Hebrews 6:4-6 does not apply to the Body of Christ.

In Hebrews chapter 8 we read:

*"For finding fault with them, he saith, Behold, the days come, saith the Lord, when I will make **a new covenant with the house of Israel and with the house of Judah**: ... For this is the covenant that I will make with the house of Israel **after those days**, saith the Lord; I will put my laws into their mind, and write them in their hearts: and I will be to them a God, and they shall be to me a people:" - Hebrews 8:8, 10*

This covenant with Israel and Judah is "after those days", the days of the Tribulation. Then the Lord will put His law into the hearts and minds of the Jews, and they will be His people. This is a reference to the Millennial kingdom of Jesus Christ. It has nothing to do with the church, the Body of Christ. We are not under the Law of Moses, so we do not need it written in our hearts.

Hebrews 8:10 is a quote from Jeremiah chapter 31.

*"But this shall be the covenant that I will make with the **house of Israel**; After those days, saith the LORD, I will put my law in their inward parts, and write it in their hearts; and will be their God, and they shall be my people." - Jeremiah 31:33*

This covenant is with Israel and fulfilled at the second coming of Jesus Christ. Since Israel at that time will be under the Law of Moses, they will finally be able to keep the Law, written in their hearts replacing their sinful nature.

This is a popular verse from chapter 10:

*"Not forsaking the assembling of ourselves together, as the manner of some is; but exhorting one another: and so much the more, **as ye see the day approaching**." - Hebrews 10:25*

Sounds like this verse could apply to the Body of Christ and many pastors use it. But there is a qualifier, "as ye see the day approaching." What day is that? The Rapture? No. In the Body of Christ, we cannot see the day of the Rapture approaching as we have no clue when that day will come. The "day approaching" is the second coming of Jesus Christ at the end of the 7-year Tribulation. Jews in the Tribulation will see that day approaching as the Tribulation is exactly 7 years long.

Another verse in Hebrews chapter 10 creates serious difficulty if erroneously applied to the Body of Christ.

*"For if we **sin wilfully** after that we have received the knowledge of the truth, there **remaineth no more sacrifice for sins**, But a certain fearful looking for of **judgment** and **fiery indignation**, which shall devour the adversaries." - Hebrews 10:26-27*

This is another verse that applies only to Israel and not to the Body of Christ. If we sin wilfully, we can confess our sin to the Lord Jesus Christ as He is faithful and just to forgive us. But if a Jew willfully sins during the 7-year Tribulation by taking the mark of the beast, his sin cannot be forgiven. He then fearfully awaits the judgment and fiery indignation from the Lord as there is no remedy for taking the mark of the beast.

Another important passage in Hebrews:

*"Lest there be any fornicator, or profane person, as Esau, who for one morsel of meat **sold his birthright**. For ye know how that afterward, when he would have inherited the blessing, **he was rejected**: for he found **no place of repentance**, though he sought it carefully with tears." - Hebrews 12:16-17*

Esau sold his birthright for a meal, but later when he sought repentance there was none, he was rejected. The same is true for a Jew in the 7-year Tribulation. If a Jew sells his birthright, inheritance of the kingdom, by taking the mark of the beast then there is no place of repentance, he will be rejected by God. We saw in chapter 6:4-6 that if they should fall away it is impossible to renew them unto repentance. A fitting example is the five foolish virgins rejected by the Lord at the marriage feast.

The book of Hebrews is remarkably interesting and contains much information that we as Christians should know. Read Hebrews again, but this time with the mindset of a Jew going through the 7-year Tribulation, you will be amazed at the clarity.

Book of James

The book of James begins with:

*"James, a servant of God and of the Lord Jesus Christ, to the **twelve tribes which are scattered abroad**, greeting." – James 1:1*

James wrote to the "twelve tribes" of Israel, not the Body of Christ. Gentiles are not "scattered abroad." Jews outside of their homeland, are considered scattered. James wrote about works, patience, and endurance. These are qualities necessary for Jews in the 7-year Tribulation as Israel is back under the Law of Moses which is a works-based approval system from God.

*"But be ye **doers** of the word, and not hearers only, deceiving your own selves. ... But whoso looketh into the perfect law of liberty, and **continueth** therein, he being not a forgetful hearer, but a **doer of the work**, this man shall be blessed in his deed." – James 1:22, 25*

James instructs Jews to be a doer of the word because during the Tribulation the Jews are under the Law of Moses. If they do not keep the Law, the Lord Jesus will reject them His second coming. They must continue in doing the Law until the end. In the body of Christ, we do not live and function as doers of the word keeping the commandments. We operate by faith, walking in the Spirit and the will of God for our lives.

*"What doth it profit, my brethren, though a man say he hath faith, and have not works? **can faith save him**?" – James 2:14*

*"Even so faith, if it hath not works, is dead, being alone. ... But wilt thou know, O vain man, that **faith without works is dead**?" – James 2:17, 20*

*"Ye see then how that **by works a man is justified**, and not by faith only." – James 2:24*

Under the Law of Moses, faith alone is insufficient. A Jew must do the works of the Law, sacrifices, feast days, and keep the commandments for salvation.

A simple test proving that the book of James does not apply to us, the church is this. James clearly states that "faith without works is dead." But Paul proclaims that faith without works is what saves your soul. For we are saved by grace through faith and not of works. The distinction is clear. The only remaining application of the book of James is for Israel during the 7-year Tribulation.

*"Be patient therefore, brethren, **unto the coming of the Lord**... Be ye also patient; stablish your hearts: for the **coming of the Lord draweth nigh**." – James 5:7-8*

The "coming of the Lord" is near to those in the Tribulation as He comes at the end of the 7 years. Only Jews in the Tribulation can know that the coming of the Lord is near. This does not apply to the Body of Christ as we do not know if the Rapture is near or yet far away.

Epistles of Peter

Peter opens his first epistle similarly to James' opening.

*"Peter, an apostle of Jesus Christ, to the **strangers scattered** throughout Pontus, Galatia, Cappadocia, Asia, and Bithynia," – 1ˢᵗ Peter 1:1*

"strangers scattered" does not refer to Gentiles in these Asia Minor provinces, as that is their home. It is Jews that are "strangers scattered" throughout the Gentile region of Asia Minor.

*"Who are kept by the power of God through faith unto salvation **ready to be revealed in the last time**." – 1ˢᵗ Peter 1:5*

Jews that follow Jesus Christ during the Tribulation do not receive their salvation upon belief as we currently do in the Body of Christ. They must continue to the end of the Tribulation to be saved. Their salvation is "ready to be revealed" at the second coming of Jesus Christ, the "last time."

Another similar verse:

*"That the **trial of your faith**, being much more precious than of gold that perisheth, though it be **tried with fire**, might be found unto praise and honour and glory **at the appearing of Jesus Christ**:" – 1ˢᵗ Peter 1:7*

During the Tribulation, the faith of Jews is tried by fire. That fire is the temptation and testing of the Tribulation. Remember the words of John the Baptist in Matthew chapter 3.

*"I indeed baptize you with water unto repentance: but he that cometh after me is mightier than I, whose shoes I am not worthy to bear: he shall **baptize you** with the Holy Ghost, and with **fire**:" - Matthew 3:11*

The baptism was the coming of the Holy Spirit in Acts chapter 2. The "fire" is the 7-year Tribulation where Israel and the world will be tried by fire.

A believing Jew receives his "honor and glory" at the "appearing of Jesus Christ", the second coming at the end of the Tribulation.

Another interesting verse is:

*"Wherefore gird up the loins of your mind, be sober, and **hope to the end for the grace** that is to be brought unto you at the **revelation of Jesus Christ**;" – 1ˢᵗ Peter 1:13*

As Christians in the Body of Christ, we do not need to "hope to the end" for grace. We receive grace the moment we trust in Christ for salvation. But Jews in the Tribulation must hope to the end. The passage also states that "grace" will come unto them at "the revelation of Jesus Christ." The revelation is the second coming of Christ at the end of the 7-year Tribulation. As Christians we do not need to wait for the second coming to receive God's grace, we have it now.

Why must the Jews in the 7-year Tribulation wait until the second coming of Jesus Christ to receive their salvation? Because they must endure the fiery trials and resist the temptation to take the mark of the beast. Taking the mark will condemn them even if they previously made a profession of faith in Christ.

Peter also writes:

*"Having your conversation honest among the Gentiles: that, whereas they speak against you as evildoers, they may by your good works, which they shall behold, glorify God in **the day of visitation**." – 1ˢᵗ Peter 2:12*

Peter was writing to Jews commanding them to be "honest among the Gentiles." That by their "good works" Gentiles might "glorify God in the day of visitation." That is the second coming of Jesus Christ at the end of the Tribulation. The second coming is the "day of visitation." Jews, setting the example of godliness for the Gentiles.

*"That ye may be mindful of the words which were spoken before by the holy **prophets**, and of the **commandment of us the apostles** of the Lord and Saviour: Knowing this first, that there shall come in the **last days scoffers**, walking after their own lusts," – 2ⁿᵈ Peter 3:2-3*

Peter is reminding Jews of the words spoken by the prophets and the apostles. This is not written to the Body of Christ, as the prophets of old knew nothing about the dispensation of grace. "Last days" is a reference to the Tribulation not the ending of the dispensation of grace with the Rapture. These scoffers are scoffing at the second coming of Jesus Christ not the Rapture of the Body of Christ as clearly seen in the next verse.

"And saying, Where is the promise of his coming? for since the fathers fell asleep, all things continue as they were from the beginning of the creation." - 2Peter 3:4

In Peter's life, the only fathers he knew were the fathers of Israel. He then states that everything continues from the beginning of creation. This is not a reference to the Rapture but the second coming of Jesus at the end of the Tribulation.

The books of 1ˢᵗ and 2ⁿᵈ Peter were written to guide and instruct Israel as they endure the fire of the 7-year Tribulation. Peter is not writing to the Body of Christ but Israel as he is an apostle to the Jews.

Epistles of John

In 1ˢᵗ, 2ⁿᵈ, and 3ʳᵈ John, the apostle John writes many times about keeping the commandments.

*"And hereby we do know that we know him, **if we keep his commandments**. He that saith, I know him, and keepeth not his **commandments**, is a liar, and the truth is not in him." – 1ˢᵗ John 2:3-4*

We in the Body of Christ know Jesus by grace through faith, not by keeping commandments. God accepts us into fellowship with Him through His Grace via our faith. The keeping of commandments was for Israel as they alone were given the Law. This is another reference to keeping the Law of Moses during the Tribulation. Once the Rapture of the Body of Christ happens, Israel is back under the Law of Moses and prophecy.

*"And whatsoever we ask, we receive of him, because **we keep his commandments**, and do those things that are pleasing in his sight." – 1ˢᵗ John 3:22*

Our prayers, in the Body of Christ, are answered by faith, not by keeping commandments.

*"For this is the love of God, that we **keep his commandments**: and his commandments are not grievous." – 1ˢᵗ John 5:3*

*"And this is love, that we **walk after his commandments**. This is the commandment, That, as ye have heard from the beginning, ye should walk in it."* – 2nd John 1:6

We show love for Jesus by walking in the Spirit, not keeping commandments.

*"If any man see his brother sin a sin which is not unto **death**, he shall ask, and he shall give him life for them that sin not unto **death**. There is a **sin unto death**: I do not say that he shall pray for it."* – 1st John 5:16

There is no "sin unto death" presently for the Body of Christ. However, there is a sin unto death during the 7-year Tribulation, taking the mark of the beast. That sin should not be prayed for as there is no remedy.

John introduces the Antichrist in his epistles. Is it coincidental this comes just before the book of Revelation that reveals much about the Antichrist and the Tribulation? I think not.

Chapter Ten – The Book of Revelation

The traditional understanding of the Book of Revelation teaches that chapters 2 and 3, the letters to the seven churches, apply to the church, the Body of Christ. Everything from chapter 4 thru 22 is future.

But do the seven letters in chapters 2 and 3 apply to the Body of Christ or future churches, or assemblies, of Jews in the 7-year Tribulation? Remember, the apostle John is an apostle to the circumcision, Israel, not the Body of Christ as is Paul.

Many clues reveal the audience of the book of Revelation is Israel enduring the Tribulation. Let's see what the scriptures say beginning with Rev 1:1.

*"**The Revelation of Jesus Christ**, which God gave unto him, to shew unto his servants things which must **shortly come to pass**; and he sent and signified it by his angel unto his servant John:"* - Revelation 1:1

The apostle John gives the context of the book in verse one; "The Revelation of Jesus Christ". The revelation of Jesus Christ is not the Rapture but the second coming at the end of the Tribulation where every eye will see him. At the revelation of Jesus Christ, He returns to save Israel, defeat the Antichrist and the enemies of God.

The events surrounding the "revelation of Jesus Christ" must "shortly come to pass." How could John make such a statement if he was aware of the dispensation of grace, God's program to save Gentiles. If John wrote the Revelation in 95 A.D. as is commonly taught, he knew Jerusalem and the Temple were destroyed and his people scattered. He would understand God's judgment was upon Israel, not the soon blessing of the kingdom. So why did he say things would "shortly come to pass?"

Chart 11 shows God's program for Israel before the revelation of the dispensation of grace via the apostle Paul.

I believe the answer is that John wrote the Revelation soon after Jesus' ascension to heaven. An early date for Revelation would answer the question. In the early chapters of Acts, Jews were looking for the return of their Messiah Jesus to set up the kingdom. They were unaware of the dispensation of grace as that came later in Acts chapter 9 with the saving of Paul. I believe an early writing for all the epistles of Peter, James, and John. This is bared out in Acts chapter 6.

*"Then the twelve called the multitude of the disciples unto them, and said, It is not reason that **we should leave the word of God** and serve tables. ... But we will give ourselves continually to prayer, and to the **ministry of the word**. ... And the **word of God increased**; and the number of the disciples multiplied in Jerusalem greatly; and a great company of the priests were obedient to the faith." - Acts 6:2, 4, 7*

The twelve disciples appointed Stephen to distribute goods and serve tables. Peter and the apostles ministered to writing the word. They wrote their epistles while others saw to the needs of the widows. The written "word of God increased" during that time as the gospels and the epistles of Peter, James and John were compiled and distributed to the believing Jews. Remember, Peter, James, and John were apostles to the Jews.

Let's continue now with the text of Revelation.

*"Blessed is he that readeth, and they that hear the **words of this prophecy**, and **keep those things** which are written therein: for the **time is at hand**." - Revelation 1:3*

In verse 3, John calls the Revelation, "words of this prophecy." Previously we saw that prophecy refers to Israel and the mystery refers to the Body of Christ. Since the book of Revelation is a prophecy, its target audience is Israel.

John also states there is a blessing for those that "keep those things which are written therein." As we study, we will see that only those going through the 7-year Tribulation can keep the things written in the book, the Body of Christ cannot.

"the time is at hand" – refers to Israel during the Tribulation as only during the Tribulation would anyone know the "time is at hand" because Jesus is returning at the end of the 7-years.

In Revelation chapter 1 we read phrases like the following concerning Jesus Christ:

- "which is, and which was, and which is to come"
- "I am Alpha and Omega, the beginning and the ending"
- "I am Alpha and Omega, the first and the last"
- "I am the first and the last"
- "I am he that liveth, and was dead; and, behold, I am alive forevermore"

These are descriptives of Jesus used only by Jews. Paul does not refer to Jesus using this type of language. They are allusions to Isaiah.

*"Hearken unto me, O Jacob and Israel, my called; I am he; **I am the first, I also am the last**." - Isaiah 48:12*

Continuing in Revelation.

*"Behold, he cometh with clouds; and **every eye shall see him**, and they also **which pierced him**: and all kindreds of the earth shall wail because of him. Even so, Amen." - Revelation 1:7*

When Jesus returns at the end of the Tribulation, "every eye shall see him." This is not the Rapture. This is the second coming at the end of the Tribulation. "They which pierced him" are the leaders of Israel, that demanded the crucifixion of Jesus. This is not a blanket reference to Israel. This could only make sense if the Book of Revelation were written shortly after the ascension of Jesus in the early chapters of Acts before Paul's conversion and the beginning of the dispensation of grace. At that time "they which pierced him" were still alive to see the second coming of Jesus 7 years later per Chart 11. Had the Jews accepted Stephen's testimony in Acts chapter 7, the 7-year Tribulation would have soon begun and those that crucified Jesus would see His return.

*"I was in the Spirit on the **Lord's day**, and heard behind me a great voice, as of a trumpet, … I am he that liveth, and was dead; and, behold, I am alive forevermore, Amen; and have the keys of hell and of death." - Revelation 1:10, 18*

The "Lord's day" refers to the Day of the Lord. This day begins with the prophesied judgment of the 7-year Tribulation and continues thru the Millennial Reign. Another clue that the audience is Israel.

The apostle John was told by Jesus to write to the seven churches that are in Asia (v. 4). The traditional teaching is that these churches are Gentile churches started by the Apostle Paul but that is not the case. In Acts chapter 2 there are Jews from the province of Asia in Jerusalem for the feast of Pentecost.

*"Parthians, and Medes, and Elamites, and the dwellers in Mesopotamia, and in Judaea, and Cappadocia, in Pontus, and **Asia**," - Acts 2:9*

These Jews believed in Jesus as Messiah, were baptized, and returned to their cities in Asia. There they started small groups with fellow believers. These believers were not members of the Body of Christ as the apostle Paul had not yet been saved. These churches, assemblies, were entirely Jewish believing in Jesus their Messiah. They are "Little Flock" churches as we saw earlier. Such will be the case after the Rapture of the Body of Christ. The abundance of believers in the Tribulation will be Jews as it is their time of redemption.

John also refers to Jesus among the candlesticks and the candlesticks are the seven churches. The apostle Paul never refers to the Body of Christ as a candlestick. Jesus calls Israel a candlestick in Matthew chapter 5:15 calling them the light of the world. During the Tribulation, they will once again be the light of the world to all that desire the truth.

Another interesting point is found in verse 13.

*"And in the midst of the seven candlesticks one like unto the **Son of man**, clothed with a garment down to the foot, and girt about the paps with a golden girdle." - Rev 1:13*

John refers to Jesus as the "Son of Man". That is because the Jews had a relationship with the man Jesus Christ during His earthly ministry. The Body of Christ has a spiritual relationship with Jesus Christ as it began several years after Jesus ascended to heaven. The apostle Paul never calls Jesus the "Son of Man" but the "Son of God". The "Son of Man" title is only for Israel.

Just from chapter one, the context is the Jews and Israel, not the Body of Christ.

Another name given to Jesus in Revelation is "Lamb." 27 times John refers to Jesus as the Lamb. Is Jesus a Lamb for the Body of Christ? No, He is the Lamb for Israel. Jesus is the "head" of the body of Christ. The concept of the Lamb harkens back to the first Passover in Egypt where the angel of death passed over the houses where the blood of the lamb was on the doorposts. The purpose of the lamb was to save Israel, not Gentiles. The "Lamb" is an entirely Jewish concept. Jesus is the Lamb of God for Israel, not Gentiles. When you read passages referring to Jesus as the Lamb, the intended audience is Israel, not the Body of Christ. Jesus is our Lord and Savior, not our Lamb or Shepherd. The apostle Paul never refers to Jesus as our Lamb.

Revelation Ch. 2 & 3

Chapters 2 & 3 present several issues that are problematic for a member of the Body of Christ believing in salvation by grace. They are as follows:

- Jesus is primarily concerned about "works". There is no mention of grace or the gospel of grace. Works indicate these believers are under the Law as the Law is a works-based performance system from God.
- Five of the seven letters contain judgment and condemnation. But the Body of Christ is not under any judgment or condemnation as Paul states in Romans 8:1. "There is therefore now no condemnation to them which are in Christ Jesus, who walk not after the flesh, but after the Spirit."
- The churches are commanded to repent, repent and repent. Paul never tells believers to repent but to believe.

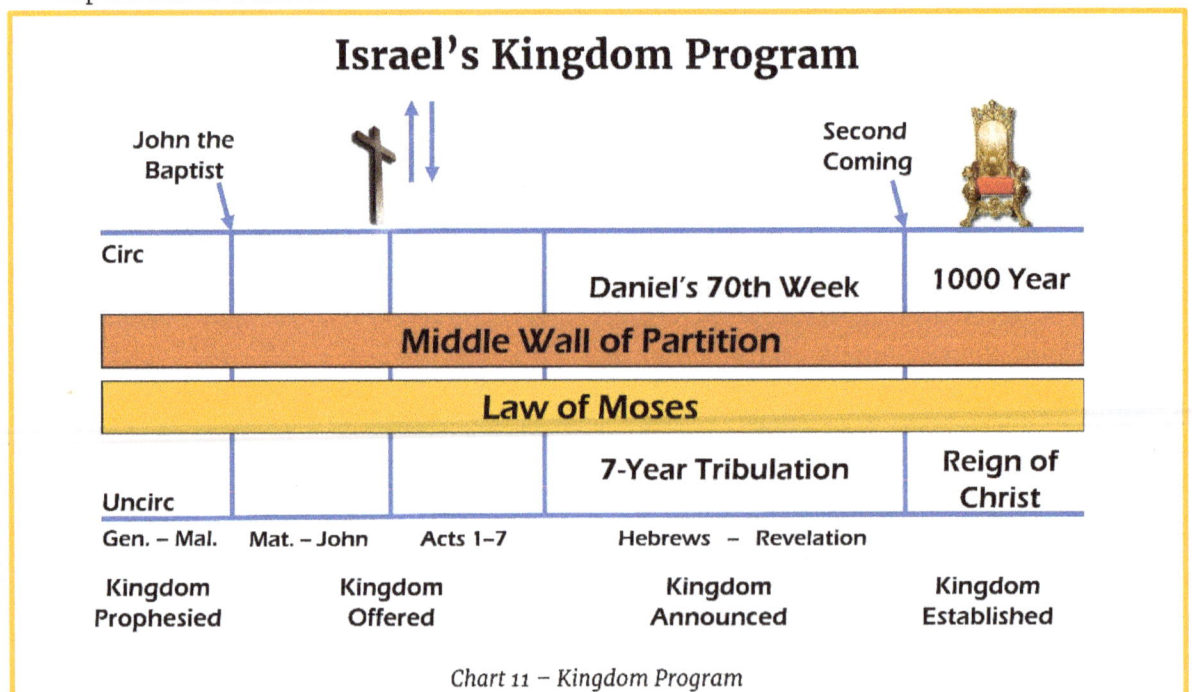

Chart 11 – Kingdom Program

- In each of the seven churches, there is a promise and blessing to the Overcomer. This concept is not found in Paul's epistles as every member of the Body of Christ is already an overcomer.
- The concept of an overcomer is found in the gospels, 2nd Peter and 1st John, the Hebrew epistles for the Tribulation period. It is a Jewish concept as they must overcome the world, the devil, and the mark of the beast.
- What Jesus spoke in the gospels and Acts was to Israel as the Body of Christ was not yet in existence. Why would Jesus address the Gentile Church in the Book of Revelation since He declared the Apostle Paul the apostle to the Gentiles? Remember, Jesus came to minister to the lost sheep of the house of Israel.

My purpose here is not to examine the entire Book of Revelation as all premillennialists agree that chapters 4 thru 22 are yet future and that chapters 6 thru 19 concern the 7-year Tribulation culminating in the second coming of Jesus Christ.

Let's do a quick review of the seven churches in Revelation chapters 2 & 3 with a question in mind. Who is the intended audience, the Jews or the Body of Christ?

The Seven Churches

The letter to each church is addressed to "the angel". Most teachers will tell you that "angel" means messenger, so the "angel" is the pastor of that church. If the Holy Spirit wanted to say "pastor", why didn't he just say "pastor"? However, He said "angel".

In Hebrews, we read concerning angels.

*"Are they not all **ministering spirits**, sent forth to minister for them who shall be **heirs of salvation**?" – Hebrews 1:14*

Angels are "ministering spirits" sent to Israel. Jews are the "heirs of salvation." They receive that salvation at the second coming of Jesus Christ at the end of the Tribulation period. The Body of Christ has no angels sent to minister to the church. We are "in Christ". Jesus Christ is in us. We are sealed with the Holy Spirit. We do not need Angels to teach or minister to us. That is the Holy Spirit's role in the Body of Christ.

The fact that these seven churches have angels over them is yet another clue that Israel, the Jews, are the intended audience. The timeframe is the 7-year Tribulation. The apostle Paul never mentions angels ministering to the Body of Christ.

The churches are called "candlesticks." Are candlesticks applicable to Israel or the Body of Christ? Let's look at scripture.

*"And thou shalt make a **candlestick** of pure gold: of beaten work shall the **candlestick** be made: his shaft, and his branches, his bowls, his knops, and his flowers, shall be of the same." – Exodus 25:31*

*"The **candlestick** also for the light, and his furniture, and his lamps, with the oil for the light," – Exodus 35:14*

*"Ye (Israel) are the light of the world. A city (Jerusalem) that is set on an hill cannot be hid. Neither do men light a candle, and put it under a bushel, but on a **candlestick**; and it giveth light unto all*

*that are in the house. Let your light so shine before men, that they may **see your good works**, and glorify your Father which is in heaven." - Matthew 5:14-16 Parenthesis mine*

- "Candlesticks," as a symbolic bearer of light is entirely a Jewish concept.
- The light of the "candlestick" is the Law, good works.

- *"For the **commandment** is a **lamp**; and the **law** is **light**; and reproofs of instruction are the way of life:" - Proverbs 6:23*

- Old Testament thru Acts 7 teaches faith + works of the Law, the gospel of the kingdom, and candlesticks.
- Romans thru Philemon teaches Grace through Faith, no works, no Law, no candlestick.
- Hebrews thru Revelation teaches the gospel of the kingdom, everlasting gospel (faith + works of the Law), candlesticks.
- The apostle Paul never associates the Body of Christ with "candlesticks".

The Church of Ephesus

Jesus commends them for their works, labor, and patience. As we have read elsewhere, works are related to Israel keeping the commandments of the Law of Moses. They were required of Jews to be accepted by God and worthy of salvation. Not so with the Body of Christ as we are saved by grace, not works. The Jews at Ephesus also have patience. They are patiently waiting for their Messiah, Jesus Christ, who will return at the end of the Tribulation.

*"Here is the **patience of the saints**: here are they that **keep the commandments of God**, and the faith of Jesus." - Revelation 14:12*

While they are patiently waiting for Jesus to return, they "keep the commandments of God." We, the Body of Christ, are not focused on keeping the commandments of God while we wait for the Rapture. We walk in the Spirit and will of God. Striving to keep the commandments of the Law of Moses is entirely Jewish. Since Gentiles were never given any Law or commandments by God. How can we be held accountable for something we never received?

Jesus rebukes the Jews at Ephesus for leaving their "first love." Seems they became more focused on works and less on Jesus, their Messiah. They must repent and return to their "first love" their Messiah. This is the same mindset of the Pharisees in the gospels. They kept the letter of the Law but not the Spirit.

The overcomer in Ephesus is promised to "eat from the tree of life." Eating from the tree of life brings eternal life. This applies to Israel, not the Body of Christ, as we already have eternal life through our Lord and Savior Jesus Christ.

*"Blessed are they (Israel) that **do his commandments**, that they may have right to the **tree of life** and may enter in through the gates into the city (the New Jerusalem)." - Revelation 22:14 parenthesis mine*

Those that eat from the tree of life must "do his commandments." Only then can they have eternal life. Jews in the Tribulation must keep the commandments. We, the Body of Christ, receive eternal life the moment we believe.

The Church of Smyrna

Something very interesting happens at Smyrna.

*"I know thy works, and tribulation, and poverty, (but thou art rich) and I know the blasphemy of them which say they are Jews, and are not, but are the **synagogue of Satan**." - Revelation 2:9*

What is the synagogue of Satan? Who are those that say they are Jews but are not? Why should we in the Body of Christ care about Jews in a synagogue? We wouldn't. In the Body of Christ, there is no Jew or Gentile. We are one new man. But since the passage singles out Jews, this cannot refer to the Body of Christ. Another clue that these seven letters are to the Jews in the Tribulation, not the Body of Christ.

Do we, the Body of Christ, care about nefarious activities in a synagogue? No! But Jews in the Tribulation would as that is where they meet. Who are those that say they are Jews but are not? Remember the Nazi collaborators from WWII. Jews that collaborated with the Nazis, betraying fellow Jews for favor with the Reich.

This will be repeated during the 7-year Tribulation. Some Jews will collaborate with the Antichrist system for favor hoping to escape death. These collaborators will reject Jesus as the Messiah and accept the Antichrist. They are not true Jews in God's eyes. Since they have aligned with the Antichrist, they are of the synagogue of Satan. This has nothing to do with the Body of Christ. Jesus gives a prophecy of this activity in the Olivet Discourse.

"And then shall many be offended, and shall betray one another, and shall hate one another." - Matthew 24:10

Jews betraying Jews because they are offended at Jesus their Messiah.

The Church of Pergamos

*"And to the angel of the church in Pergamos write; These things saith he which hath the **sharp sword with two edges**;" - Revelation 2:12*

Jesus with a "sharp sword" depicts judgment and condemnation, not grace and peace.

*"And out of his mouth goeth a **sharp sword**, that with it he should **smite the nations**: and he shall rule them with a **rod of iron**: and he treadeth the winepress of the **fierceness and wrath** of Almighty God." - Revelation 19:15*

No one in their right mind wants to be on the receiving end of Jesus' sharp sword. That sharp sword is for a Christ-rejecting Israel and the kingdom of the Antichrist. Jesus will use that sharp sword when He returns at the end of the 7-year Tribulation.

The apostle Paul never mentions the "sharp sword" concerning the Body of Christ. Would Jesus take a sharp sword to His own Body? That's absurd, I think not.

Those at Pergamos have a problem with a group named Nicolaitans.

*"So hast thou also them that hold the doctrine of the Nicolaitans, which thing I hate. Repent; or else **I will come unto thee quickly and will fight against them with the sword of my mouth**." - Revelation 2:15-16*

Best guess is Nicolaitans represent a hierarchy of authoritarian leadership over believers. Jesus hates that, He wants believers to come directly to Him. No intermediary clergy is necessary. Jesus instructs those at Pergamos to repent. If they do not, He will come quickly and fight with the sword of His mouth, the Word.

This cannot apply to the Body of Christ as Jesus is not coming quickly to fight with His body. When Jesus comes at the Rapture there is no fighting just rejoicing that we are finally going home. But when Jesus returns at the second coming, He comes to judge, and make war. He comes to fight against His enemies. He comes to save true Israel.

The overcomer at Pergamos will eat hidden manna and receive a white stone with a new name written on it. Paul never uses this type of language about the Body of Christ. We are not promised a new name on a white stone. This is entirely Jewish. Manna refers to Israel wandering in the wilderness being fed by God. In Isaiah, we read.

*"For Zion's sake will I not hold my peace, and for Jerusalem's sake I will not rest, until the righteousness thereof go forth as brightness, and the salvation thereof as a lamp that burneth. And the **Gentiles** shall see thy righteousness, and all kings thy glory: and **thou shalt be called by a new name**, which the mouth of the LORD shall name." - Isaiah 62:1-2*

It is all about Israel and their Messiah.

The Church of Thyatira

*"And unto the angel of the church in Thyatira write; These things saith the Son of God, who hath his eyes like unto a **flame of fire**, and his feet are like **fine brass**;" - Revelation 2:18*

The letter to the Jews at Thyatira opens describing Jesus with eyes like a flame of fire and feet of fine brass. This description portends judgment. When Jesus returns at the end of the Tribulation, He comes to judge and make war.

*"And I saw heaven opened, and behold a white horse; and he that sat upon him was called Faithful and True, and in righteousness he doth **judge and make war**." - Revelation 19:11*

For the Body of Christ, any judgment due us was paid in full by Jesus on the cross. We are the recipients of grace, not judgment. Sure, the Holy Spirit will convict us of sin and guide us to the will of God. But grace and judgment are mutually exclusive. Grace cancels judgment. Not so for Israel during the Tribulation.

The believers at Thyatira tolerate a prophetess named Jezebel. The original Jezebel in scripture is from 1st Kings. She was a Gentile who worshipped Baal and Ashtaroth. Her punishment then was to be eaten by dogs. This prophetess in Thyatira suffers a different and unique fate.

*"And I gave her space to repent of her fornication; and she repented not. Behold, I will cast her into a bed, and them that commit adultery with her **into great tribulation**, except they repent of their deeds." – Revelation 2:21-22*

She and her followers are told to repent, but they do not. Their punishment is to be cast into "great tribulation." This is a reference to the last half of the 7-year Tribulation spoken by Jesus.

*"For then shall be **great tribulation**, such as was not since the beginning of the world to this time, no, nor ever shall be." - Matthew 24:21*

Those martyred during the last half of the Tribulation are spoken of in Revelation chapter 7.

*"And I said unto him, Sir, thou knowest. And he said to me, These are they which came out of **great tribulation**, and have washed their robes, and made them white in the blood of the Lamb." - Revelation 7:14*

This pertains to Jews in the 7-year Tribulation. No one in the Body of Christ will ever be cast into the "great tribulation."

*"**And I will kill her children with death**; and all the churches shall know that I am he which searcheth the reins and hearts: and I will give unto every one of you according to your works." - Revelation 2:23*

I always found that phrase puzzling. It seems redundant to kill someone with death. Then I remembered the 4th horseman of Revelation chapter 6.

*"And I looked and behold a pale horse: and his name that sat on him was **Death**, and Hell followed with him. And power was given unto them over the fourth part of the earth, to kill with sword, and with hunger, and with death, and with the beasts of the earth." - Revelation 6:8*

The name of the pale horse rider is Death. He kills so many people during the 7-year Tribulation that Hell follows close to quickly gather the souls of the dead. The followers of Jezebel during the Tribulation will be killed by the horse rider named Death. Now the phrase makes sense.

Another interesting passage to the believers at Thyatira refers to Satan.

*"But unto you I say, and unto the rest in Thyatira, as many as have not this doctrine, and which have not known the **depths of Satan**, as they speak; I will put upon you none other burden. But that which ye have already hold fast till I come." - Revelation 2:24-25*

How does one come to know the depths of Satan? Can we, the Body of Christ, know the depths of Satan? No. The depths of Satan can only be known after Satan is kicked out of heaven to the earth. When Satan is here on earth unleashing his wrath because his time is short. This happens in Revelation chapter 12 in the middle of the 7-year Tribulation.

*"And the great dragon was cast out, that old serpent, called the Devil, and Satan, which deceiveth the whole world: he was **cast out into the earth**, and his angels were cast out with him." - Revelation 12:9*

The "depths of Satan" are fully manifest during the last half of the Tribulation. Another strong clue that the letters to the seven churches are for Jewish believers during the Tribulation.

The believers at Thyatira are commanded to hold on to the end.

*"And he that overcometh, and **keepeth my works unto the end**, to him will I give power over the nations: And he **shall rule them with a rod of iron**; as the vessels of a potter shall they be broken to shivers: even as I received of my Father." - Revelation 2:26-27*

The Jewish believers during the Tribulation are operating under the Law of Moses. That's why there is so much focus on keeping the commandments and works. Those at Thyatira are to keep the works of the Lord "unto the end." Either the end of their life if they are martyred or the end of the Tribulation, whichever comes first.

There is a similar verse in the Olivet Discourse saying the same thing.

*"But he that shall **endure unto the end**, the same shall be saved." - Matthew 24:13*

Tribulation Jews must endure.

The Church of Sardis

Sardis has an interesting verse about the thief in the night.

*"Remember therefore how thou hast received and heard, and hold fast, and repent. If therefore thou shalt not watch, **I will come on thee as a thief**, and thou shalt not know what hour I will come upon thee." - Revelation 3:3*

Paul mentions a thief in the night in 1 Thessalonians chapter 5 concerning the Day of the Lord.

*"For yourselves know perfectly that the **day of the Lord so cometh as a thief in the night**. For when they shall say, Peace and safety; then **sudden destruction** cometh upon them, as travail upon a woman with child; and **they shall not escape**. But ye, brethren, are not in darkness, that that day should overtake you as a thief." – 1ˢᵗ Thessalonians 5:2-4*

The Day of the Lord comes as a thief in the night upon the whole world. With it comes "sudden destruction" and all that dwell upon the earth will not escape because they are in darkness. Paul adds that the Body of Christ is not in darkness. We will not be overtaken by the Day of the Lord, the 7-year Tribulation. The Body of Christ is caught up to the Lord in the clouds before the Tribulation.

The "thief in the night" concept refers to the second coming of Jesus Christ. Most in the world will not be expecting His return at the end of the 7-year Tribulation.

Church of Philadelphia

*"And to the angel of the church in Philadelphia write; These things saith he that is holy, he that is true, he that hath the **key of David**, he that openeth, and no man shutteth; and shutteth, and no man openeth;" - Revelation 3:7*

Notice that Jesus has the "Key of David". Jesus controls who enters the Kingdom and who does not. To some it will be open, to others it will be shut. We see this portrayed in the parable of the ten virgins.

*"Then shall the **kingdom of heaven** be likened unto ten virgins, which took their lamps, and went forth to meet the bridegroom. And five of them were **wise**, and five were **foolish**. They that were foolish took their lamps and took no oil with them: But the wise took oil in their vessels with their lamps. While the bridegroom tarried, they all slumbered and slept." - Matthew 25:1-5*

This parable is about the "kingdom of heaven," the Millennial Reign of Jesus Christ on earth. Jesus and John the Baptist spoke about the kingdom of heaven during their ministries. This is an earthly kingdom promised to Israel. The ten virgins are Jews coming to meet the bridegroom just before His return. Five were prepared with enough oil for their lamps, but five were foolish not bringing enough oil.

*"And at midnight there was a cry made, Behold, the **bridegroom cometh**; go ye out to meet him. Then all those virgins arose, and trimmed their lamps. And the foolish said unto the wise, **Give us of your oil**; for our lamps are gone out. But the wise answered, saying, Not so; lest there be not enough for us and you: but **go ye rather to them that sell, and buy for yourselves**." - Matthew 25:6-9*

This is where the parable gets interesting. The coming of the bridegroom is announced. All ten virgins arise and trim their lamps. However, the foolish virgins ran out of oil. They ask the five wise virgins for some of their oil, but they refuse. The wise virgins tell the foolish virgins to go to town. There they can buy oil from those that sell. This is the key to the parable.

The setting is the 7-year Tribulation just before Jesus' second coming. What must a person have to buy and sell?

*"And he causeth all, both small and great, rich and poor, free and bond, to **receive a mark** in their right hand, or in their foreheads: And that **no man might buy or sell, save he that had the mark**, or the name of the beast, or the number of his name." - Revelation 13:16-17*

No one can buy or sell unless they have the mark of the beast. The five foolish virgins took the mark of the beast so they could buy oil for their lamps.

*"And while they went to buy, the bridegroom came; and they that were ready went in with him to the marriage: and the **door was shut**. Afterward came also the other virgins, saying, Lord, Lord, open to us. But he answered and said, Verily I say unto you, I know you not." - Matthew 25:10-12*

When the foolish virgins returned to meet the bridegroom he had already come and the door to the marriage, the kingdom, was shut. While they were away buying oil the door to the kingdom was open and the five wise virgins entered. The five foolish virgins called out to the Lord to open the door. Jesus' response is "I know you not." The five foolish virgins forfeited their inheritance in the kingdom by taking the mark of the beast. Their fate in the lake of fire is sure. Jesus has the key; he controls who enters.

I have heard many ridiculous attempts at explaining the parable of the ten virgins. The problem arises when one tries to apply this parable to the Body of Christ. It has nothing to do with the Body of Christ. It is all about Israel in the Tribulation. Since Jesus has the Key of David, He opens the kingdom for some and closes the door for others. He decides who gets in and who is left out. No one having the mark of the beast will enter. The earthly kingdom is for Israel, not the Body of Christ.

The synagogue of Satan is mentioned again. The Jews at Philadelphia have the same problem as those at Smyrna, Antichrist collaborators.

*"Behold, I will make them of the **synagogue of Satan**, which say they are Jews, and are not, but do lie;" - Revelation 3:9*

The next verse is frequently applied to the church:

*"Because thou hast kept the word of my patience, I also will **keep thee from the hour of temptation**, which shall come upon all the world, to try them that dwell upon the earth." - Revelation 3:10*

Many students of prophecy claim this is the Rapture when the church is removed from the earth, spared from the hour of temptation. Since these letters are written to Jewish assemblies in the Tribulation, this cannot refer to the Body of Christ. It refers to Jews that are protected by God during the last half of the Tribulation. They are protected in the wilderness for 3 ½ years.

*"And the woman fled into the wilderness, where she hath a **place prepared of God**, that they should feed her there a **thousand two hundred and threescore days**." - Revelation 12:6*

God prepares a place for the remnant of Israel, the woman, in the wilderness. Many believe this to be Petra in Jordan. There the remnant is protected from Satan and his Antichrist for 1260 days, 3 ½ years. This is the correct understanding of the passage to the church of Philadelphia. T be kept from the hour of temptation is not the Rapture as many believe. It is God protecting the believing remnant of Israel.

Church of Laodicea

About six miles north of Laodicea is Hierapolis. In Roman times and today, a famous health resort noted for its hot springs. Eleven miles east of Laodicea is Colossae, noted for its cold mountain streams. Both the hot springs of Hierapolis and the cold streams of Colossae were refreshing and useful to residents. Nothing like a hot bath in winter or a cold glass of water in the heat of summer.

Laodicea had an aqueduct system bringing water from both locations. But by the time the water reached Laodicea, it was lukewarm. The hot water had cooled, and the cold water warmed. The waters had lost their usefulness now being tepid.

The believers in Laodicea will be the same. They will lose their usefulness to God during the 7-year Tribulation. Lukewarm water is not refreshing being neither hot nor cold. Jesus will vomit these lukewarm believers out of His mouth. They are of no use to Him as they have acquiesced to the world systems.

*"So then because thou art **lukewarm**, and neither cold nor hot, **I will spue thee out of my mouth**." - Rev 3:16*

Proclaiming themselves to be rich and needing nothing, they bost of their self-sufficiency. They do not need the Lord.

*"Because thou sayest, I am rich, and increased with goods, and **have need of nothing**; and knowest not that thou art wretched, and miserable, and poor, and blind, and naked:" - Rev 3:17*

The Laodiceans are deceived, believing they are doing well because they have money. Sound familiar? But the Lord's opinion of them is the opposite. The Lord prospered them, but they began to rely on their prosperity instead of the Lord. Their soul became lean of the things of God.

Jesus instructs them to by "gold tried in the fire." Gold is symbolic of holiness. Believers set apart for the Lord, wholly devoted to Him. The fire in this context is the 7-year Tribulation.

*"I counsel thee to buy of me **gold tried in the fire**, that thou mayest be rich; and white raiment, that thou mayest be clothed, and that the shame of thy nakedness do not appear; and anoint thine eyes with eye salve, that thou mayest see." – Revelation 3:18*

They need to repent and stand for their Messiah Jesus. Then they will feel the fiery trials that purify the gold of holiness. Another example of an assembly, church, of believers in the Tribulation. If they do not repent, they will be cut off, spued out, from their Messiah and His Kingdom. Paul never used this type of language about the Body of Christ.

Summary

The crux of the issue is this. Do chapters 2 & 3, the letters to the seven churches, apply to the Body of Christ? No, they do not. Chapters 2 & 3 apply to churches, assemblies of Jewish believers in Jesus their Messiah, during the Tribulation. They do not apply to us today.

As you continue your study of the books of Hebrews thru Revelation, read them from the mindset of a Jew going through the 7-year Tribulation. This will bring much clarity to your understanding of scripture. The contradictions between John's writings and Paul's epistles will disappear as you discover they are written to two different audiences. John is an apostle to Israel. Paul is the apostle to the Body of Christ.

Answer to the basic questions.

1. Who is speaking? In the Hebrew epistles of Hebrews thru Revelation, the primary voice is the Holy Spirit speaking through Peter, James, and John, apostles to Israel, the Jews.
2. Who is the intended audience? Israel, the Jews, not the Body of Christ.
3. What is the timeframe or setting? The only remaining timeframe for these books is the 7-year Tribulation wherein God turns His attention back to Israel to fulfill the last day's prophecy.

Chapter Eleven – Conclusion

1. The Old Testament was written to the Jews. Its focus is Israel, Jerusalem, and Jews under the Law of Moses. We, the Body of Christ, need to have a working knowledge of the Old Testament for without it you cannot understand the Bible. However, we do not derive the Body of Christ doctrine from the Old Testament.
2. Jesus' earthly ministry recorded in Matthew thru John was to Israel under the Law, not the Body of Christ under grace. The setting in the four gospels is the same as the Old Testament—Israel, Jerusalem, the Temple, the priesthood, sacrifices, feast days, and sabbaths. We must understand the gospels as only then can we rightly divide the word of truth.
3. Acts chapters 1-7 pertain to the Jews, there's not a Gentile in sight. The middle wall of partition between Jew and Gentile has not yet been broken down. Therefore, the Body of Christ did not begin in Acts chapter 2, but later in Acts chapter 9 with the conversion of Saul, our apostle Paul.
4. Acts chapters 8 through 28 documents the diminishing of Israel and the growth of the dispensation of Grace, the Body of Christ.

5. Paul is the apostle to the Gentiles; he alone has written church doctrine for the Body of Christ in Romans thru Philemon.
6. The writings of James, Peter, and John in the books of Hebrews thru Revelation are to Israel. These men were apostles to the Jews instructing about the time of Jacob's trouble, the 7-year Tribulation.

I am not saying that we should study only Romans thru Philemon. We should study the entire Bible developing a working knowledge of it; only then can we rightly divide God's word. But always understand the intended audience of each book. Be careful not to take passages from books of the Bible written to Israel and apply them to the Body of Christ. The more knowledge you have of the Bible, the more rewarding right division will become.

The only gospel for the dispensation of Grace.

"Moreover, brethren, I declare unto you the gospel which I preached unto you, which also ye have received, and wherein ye stand; By which also ye are saved, if ye keep in memory what I preached unto you unless ye have believed in vain. For I delivered unto you, first of all, that which I also received, how that Christ died for our sins according to the scriptures; And that he was buried, and that he rose again the third day according to the scriptures:" – 1st Corinthians 15:1-4

Believe and trust what Jesus did on the cross to cleanse you from sin and restore your fellowship with the Father. Don't put your soul at risk, believe the Truth.

Anyone that does not preach this gospel is cursed.

"But though we, or an angel from heaven, preach any other gospel unto you than that which we have preached unto you, let him be accursed. As we said before, so say I now again, If any man preach any other gospel unto you than that ye have received, let him be accursed." - Galatians 1:8-9

God Bless,

Paul Felter

The End

www.ingramcontent.com/pod-product-compliance
Lightning Source LLC
Chambersburg PA
CBHW041426040426
42443CB00021B/3501